Undertow Overtures
Larry Crist

20 years of collected poetry

to
Steve
& Elyse
4/27/14
I want
that
My Body Rules
Book

ATOM Press
Mercer Island, Washington

ATOM Press
2452 - 60th Ave SE
Mercer Island, WA 98040
www.accomplishtheimpossible.com

ISBN 978-0-9842405-6-2

Library of Congress Control Number 2014935173

Printed on Acid-free paper
Cover Design by Duane Kirby Jensen
First Edition

To my younger self.

Contents

Nature & natural crimes

Literary quite contrary

Most of these poems have been previously published in: Open Sound, SkyLark, Insomnia, CrowBait, Slipstream, Silent Skies, Poetry Motel, Spitting Image, Raven Chronicles, Eureka Magazine, 4th Street, Anthology, Poets West, Snow Monkey, Pontoon, Spleen Quarterly, Above and Below, Lucid Stone, Chrysanthemum Magazine, Touched by Eros, Stray Dog, Curbside Review, California Quarterly, Pinball Publishing: Eye-rhyme, Real Change—Seattle's Homeless Newspaper, Rattle, Roarshock, Stringtown, Steam Ticket, Heliotrope, Buckle&, Red Rock Review, Artisan, Phantasmagoria, Pearl, Karamu, Alimentum, Rogue, When it Rains From the Ground Up, Red Hawk Review, Common Ground Review, Nerve Cowboy, Four Corners, Freshwater, Arch & Quiver, Cadillac Cicatrix, Colere, Hurricane Review, Midway Journal, Dos Passos Review, Tapestries, Floating Bridge Review, J Journal, The Taylor Trust, Minnetonka Review, Evening Street Review, Willow Springs, Bluestem, Your Hands, Your Mouth, Clover, Santa Fe Review, The Walrus, Blue Collar Review, JellyFish Whispers, Randomly Accessed Poetics, The Cape Rock, Kind of a Hurricane, The Creekside, The Far Field.

1
Early atrocities

Holding on

We had all been on it
The best ride ever
for money or free
It overlooked a valley
—Mill Valley, California
where we all lived

Who put it up, or how
we never knew, but a fishing pole
was needed to reel it in
You grasping for the end knot
with feet anchored
in a tangle of roots
a trusted friend
holding you by your belt
lest you slip

With knot in hand
you took a deep breath
kicked backward
and you were off
as if shot from a gun
over the slope
high above redwoods and pine

That town we knew in the distance—
the cinema, our school, the giant
Catholic Church, the record store and ice cream shop. . .
and all those roads connecting our there
to here and our here to this—this end of rope

Your eyes teared-up, knuckles
white, nails gouged your hands
though you dared not loosen them
Nothing below for hundreds of feet
racing toward that weightless
divide—you on a rope like a bar of soap
racing over your existence

holding on

Before the return—the all-critical return
Your friends
a football field away
there, without you
speeding back
like an arrow
back
to that tangle of roots

They grabbed you, as the next
took the knot, that next
daredevil
in the lot
The best ride ever
the best i ever tested
and in turn, tested you

until, not long after, one of us lost his grip, his lease
on this life, anyway, his who-knew-what. . .
complete at twelve years old, testing this
that terrified us all

He went on without us
As we continued on

They took the rope down after this

As we continued on

Milk

The hot splash of milk in the cold pail
Steam rises as the philosopher's hands find rhythm
The goat no longer bleating, silently braced
With every tug a different sound
resounding through the aluminum pail
The lamp casting upward shadows on spider beams
across the philosopher's face and glasses
making this morning routine appear sinister

He starts every day this way
The goats don't care if it's sunday or monday or Christmas morn
They need to be milked
and maybe he needs to milk them
He can throw I Ching and do Tai Chi later
while the hot milk cools he can meditate and hover
down divine imponderable avenues
and when he returns
there will be milk
good rich milk
thick as oil

He never had a mother
he never tasted her milk
Goat's milk for him was an acquired taste
maybe it wasn't even good for him
but for me it was essential

And when he left
and the goats were gone
i could tell the difference
every time we went to the store
and bought its pasteurized fortified reduced fat substitute
milked by machine from unseen cows
fresh from the carton and dated so we'd know

My philosopher father had transcended
these earthly ties
and the milk no longer flowed
nor would ever be the same

Goats

Come spring i'd have new playmates
The nannies lapped at the afterbirth
spread rich like liver upon the rain soaked grass
The newborns took their first steps
fell, got licked, rose, stood, stepped, fell again
learning everything a goat needed to know
inside that first week
Following mom and her dangling nipples
her protruding sack
staked by chain and eating everything within its radius
The kids, one, two, sometimes three
stayed close to the teat
as mom endured
eating constantly
to keep her strength up

That goat's milk was high octane stuff
and when i was forced to give up goats for people
goat's milk for common cow's
the goat remained
inside my bones, my skin, my unyielding stubborn weed-filled head
their bleating cries
their single-minded purpose

There was my favorite billy
who would climb atop our black Buick
his long white hair fragrant with piss
He'd throw back his bearded horny head
stomp a hoof upon the roof
laugh and bleat at the sun
in sharp minor chords
like he knew something
the rest of us were scared to admit

No Santa

My father never told me there was no Santa
He told me of Satan though
of hell and Dante's visit there
He told me about the atom bomb
how we had dropped two on Japan
how people were vaporized leaving only a shadow
and that those were the lucky ones
He never took me to see Mary Poppins
instead we attended grainy black and white films
with subtitles and no cartoons
where women's breast
generated little excitement
He read me Animal Farm
explaining it wasn't really about animals
He told me about Vietnam
and how we were losing this war
We were losing this war the same way
the Brits first lost to us
The present history makers, he said
don't know their history
He'd take me out at night
and we'd look up at the sky
and he'd say what we were seeing
had already long since passed
and maybe somewhere
at that very moment
there was a father and son pointing our direction
a million years
this way or that
He never told me there was no Santa
but given the aforementioned
i put it together
and come Christmas
good or bad
i knew
there'd be something under the tree
whether Santa brought it
or dad had left it behind

The New stove

A mummified bat
falls from the wall out a plate-covered hole
removed to connect the new blue stove pipe
a shiny brand-spankin' new Franklin stove
clean one moment, blazing red the next
no one had to tell me not to touch it

While the people next-door had acquired a new station-wagon
and those across the vineyard sea had a new green tractor
and the ones up on the hill
whose veranda
looked down over our valley basin
and owned everything they saw
we had heat

Blazing, hot, angry beautiful heat
the gooey pitch
crackling like ornery popcorn
raging like the power of the sun
and we gathered round like the family we still were
and watched
as rain began to pelt
our single-paned windows
plop-plop-plopping in every pot or pan
scattered around the house

we had heat

Outside
the skeletal trees
scratched against the house
waved their limbs
and sighed

Next door

they had lots of kids
and no goats
Next-door they got channel 7 and had a color tv
The Jetsons, Flintstones, Johnny Quest
everything worthwhile was on channel 7
Next-door Mrs. Newman made white toast with butter & cinnamon
and did not dole out sugar
like it would rot your teeth
Next-door was where i so often wanted to be
and was
In that gigantic sprawling house
with the three-quarter veranda
where we played with legos & lincoln logs
& multi-national armymen
with hedges and vines and a lawn
with no dandelions that Mr. Newman kept mowed
or had the boys do
for he was always away
and on the rare occasion he was not
that was when i was sent home

I cut back through their yard into our's
where the goats did not look up from the grass
where my father stood naked in the kitchen
opening a can of beans
spam sizzling
a copy of Nietzsche
clasped in his armpit
a 3 day green sheen on his face
pushing up his horn-rims
asking
you hungry?

My Parents

were so very serious
He wanted to change the world
She wanted to save it
She took him on 'cuz she believed in him
He wanted her. . .
well, because she believed in him

He would have been bigger than Hitler
had he only known how
She was naive and altruistic
Neither of them ever laughed
and why should they

She wanted justice for all
and he. . .
well, maybe he didn't know either
something to do with truth
perhaps just defining the term
in any case
as their lone representative
and only tangible creation
i remember thinking
at an unbearably young age
they were weird
and not because they were parents
or even my parents
they were weird as people

Naturally i rebelled
i became a comedian
in defense
a dreamer by necessity
I dreamt we were in a big sit-com
and none of this was going on
and some couple years later
our show got cancelled

Pine box derby

Another cruel indignity foisted upon me this time through cub scouts
my pine box racer
they all look the same out of the box
mine remained the same
until the day before the big race
when i remembered i was supposed to do something to it
I sanded the edges down some
and painted it black
flat black
the kind they use in theatres to make things disappear

My mother attended race night with me
the only single mother in a sea of mothers and fathers
but mostly fathers
fathers with power tools and sanders and high gloss paint
and, perhaps allowing their sons to touch their racers for the first time
each boy placed his racer on the wooden downward track

I lined mine up among the others
many of which had decals and numbers to distinguish them
Mine required no such superficiality
it stood there like a crow among peacocks
an Edsel among Porsches
like a guilty man among the innocent

The gate rose and these little cars
succumbed to gravity and aerodynamics
and greased wheels and
well
mine was out in the first round
There was no prize for originality
or minimalism
I took my racer from the track
I wanted to light it on fire and send it
down a dark San Franciscan hill
I didn't though
I don't remember what i did with it
now to forget the rest as easily

Fight lessons

Don't grip your thumbs
don't hold them on top like that
cross 'em over your knuckles.
Keep your guard up
Think defense with your left
offense with your right.
Fake with your right
strike with your left.
Keep 'em guessing
make 'em guess wrong.
Don't stand flat-footed.
Bend your knees
launch from your legs
don't get thrown off-balance.
Remember, attitude is everything
first strike
everything else.
Hate your opponent
look 'em in the eye.
HATE THEM.
For god sake, don't bite your tongue.
Don't cry and don't fight dirty
unless you know you can get away with it.
A smart mouth will get you into it.
A good stance could get you out of it.
Cowardice will haunt you forever.
Protect your nose.
You have such a pretty nose
just like your mother's.
Never let your guard down
and never give up
keep your pretty nose pretty.

Okay, i'll see you next week.
I love you.

My old man's old man

I never met him
never even saw a photograph
No one thought it a good idea
to show me his mug-shot

The one time i saw my father in a suit
he was on his way
to the old man's funeral

My mother said he was a nice man
That the devil doth wear a pleasing face
has never
been in her thinking

He may well have been a nice man
to have been trusted with all that money
back when Dillinger and Bonnie & Clyde
produced bigger headlines and less cash

My old man's old man
toured the country
using a sundry of names
supporting my father from afar

I don't know if he ever fired a gun
kept multiple wives or girlfriends
or what
aside from what here is set down
But it must have taken
one hell of a guy
to have gotten my father
to wear that suit
with a tie that tight

On-base drinking percentage

I'm uncertain as to whether baseball
got me drinking
or drinking drew me closer to baseball

I went from not drinking and playing
to playing and drinking
to drinking and watching
to not playing at all

I played in several beer leagues
We played a lot and drank a lot
sometimes after, sometimes during

With beerball it's not whether you win or lose
It's how you drink that matters

My father introduced me to the game
drinking in his chair with me on the floor
He explained everything involved
except for the crucial enhancement of drinking while watching
which i discovered by watching him watch it

He'd lob a white plastic baseball
that i'd swing at with a red plastic bat
with a neighbor kid or two, fielding

The frantic race between plum and apple tree and back
with my dog chasing round
beamed by the ball, as good as an out

I admire the game's symmetry
try and recall whatever became of that glove i massaged with oil
or that bottle-neck bat i never quite grew large enough for

Dream of that which i can never return to
and all that i have left behind
Remembering dad
where the beer cans flew
and the hits kept coming

The Fantastic Four

were family
and behaved like family
albeit a comic book family
Ben Grimm, Reed Richards, Sue Richards & Johnny Storm
Reed was married to Sue
who was sister to Johnny
the perennial fiery teenager
who was always sparring with Ben
The Thing
science chum of Reed's

They had been struck by a cosmic radioactive something or other
on a trip to the moon
which affected them all differently
giving them their powers

I liked imagining how their powers affected their genitalia
Reed Richards could stretch his cock like an engorged anaconda
and then make it disappear in Sue Richard's invisible snatch
Johnny could make his cock burst into flames
or shoot fire
that would have been fun at the clap clinic
With his orange bricky body Ben's thing
would have been a whole 'nother thing
His petite girlfriend, Alicia
who conveniently was blind
would have had no trouble
finding her Thing
in the dark

There was always so much more to them
than their monthly 20 pages allowed
as they battled Doc Oc and Doctor Doom
the Sub Mariner and the Hulk
the Mole People, The Watcher, The Silver Surfer
all the many cosmological catastrophic cataclysms
that might face any family
saving the world and universe

again and again
practically every issue
just as weird and fucked-up as any Tolstoyian family
but staying together
a family unit
dysfunctional, yes, but working through it

The most incredible and fantastic
farfetched plot device of them all

The Girls upstairs

and i sometimes played house
or secret agents or whatever
was on tv we couldn't get enough of
Annie was a year older, and Debbie a year
younger, and Monica light years beyond us all
and was always nicer to me than her sisters
and would say hello and wave on her way out
dressed in tall shoes, short skirts, stiff hair & make-up
greeted by straight looking boys in their father's elegant cars

Annie owned little statues of Davy Jones &
Bobby Sherman & Ringo Starr and subscribed
to 17 Magazine and TeenBeat and owned a hi-fi
she played 45s on with a record changing arm
she could pile up the latest that kept dropping
playing one saccharine tune after the next

I loved Annie, and maybe Debbie loved me, and we all
admired Monica, and at night when i was sent home
to our small basement apartment where i lived with my
newly divorced mother who was seldom ever there
where i would ignore my homework and draw pictures
of superheroes and watch tv while listening for my mother
driving up so i could hop into bed and pretend to be asleep
i would often hear Mr & Mrs Mann upstairs
Mr. Mann would shout and Mrs. Mann would scream or
cry and sometimes i'd hear something break or a loud crack
followed by more sobbing, and i'd worry about the girls, and
whether Monica had come home, or what Annie or Debbie
did while their father yelled and their mother cried and
threw things, and i'd think about my parents
and how they had never fought like the Manns

Mrs. Mann emerging in the gray morning
wearing dark glasses, hours after Mr. Mann had left for work
with Annie and Debbie heading out for school shortly after
when i would try and catch up
so we could all walk together in silence

The Paperboys

Up before dawn
before the birds
helping my friend with his paper route

Drinking coffee for the first time
like i'd seen it done
black, the manly way

Reading the fresh newsprint
as we rolled the papers
it clinging to our fingers
wrapping each with a little rubber band

Speaking in whispers
filling one canvas bag
then another
taking turns by the heater
trapping the warmth in our clothes

Opening the front door
faint light visible above the trees
birds begin to notice
a rooster from somewhere
won't shut-up

With cloudy exhalations
we pretend to smoke
move toward where our bikes sit
flip up the kick-stands and began to ride

as old and young as we will ever be

Thinking of Marilyn

The first time we were in the San Francisco Wax Museum
and my mother said after i had asked, *She's considered to be*
the most beautiful woman in the world.
I thought that was Elizabeth Taylor, i said.
Depends on who you ask. Marilyn's dead, Liz is still alive.

One of the first photographs i ever jacked-off to
was from Life Magazine. Marilyn appeared to be naked
with a long leg showing and her arms and face gazing
into the camera, braced upon the pool side, a still
from her last movie that would never see release
Good porn was tough to get when i was 12 years old
I never sought out any good pics of Liz Taylor though

I remember reading that Marilyn liked to let her
lovers stay on her for as long as possible. She would wear
their love sometimes for days. Just like i wear yours today
like tungsten steel underwear, around my cock and balls
around my heart, this little i have and want to keep
close and personal for as long as possible, that which
no one can take until i willingly give it away

As for this icon who died back when i was five, i understand her
for this at least—completely. And sorry Liz, but it never was
the kind of contest any sane woman would ever try and win

Shame

We are in a restaurant:
my mother and
new step-father
I am 13 or 14 and order
2 glasses of milk
which prompts my new professorial father figure to say to the waitress:

Better bring out the whole cow.

I swear i will never eat
anywhere with him again

I order a third glass of milk
with dessert
brace for another moo
from across the table

He picks up the check

I swallow my milk
and everything else
as well

Christmas '69, Mill Valley, California

My grandfather, mother & me
Beatles White Album, my big score
I play it on my portable high-fi record player
get down on the floor
in the corner by the door
with my ear against the speaker

My grandfather, who enjoys Lawrence Welk
and my mother, who likes Pete Seeger
begin to argue
They argue a lot
usually after the evening news
after Walter Cronkite tells us how many died
that day or week

My mother argues like a mother
irrational, emotional
cries easily, shrieks on occasion

My grandfather is just a prick
He has difficulty with discussion
His impulse is to out shout his opponent
He served his country
but really his country served him
he went to Annapolis
got sunk in Pearl Harbor
retired
and began his second career
as a fucking asshole

Like any mother with an only child
my mother doesn't want to see me go to war
the fact i still have 7 years
does little to quell her hysteria

The White Album is very weird
aside from Back in the USSR
it barely rocks
and Revolution #9????
Having twice been told to turn it down
i shut it off

I rise from the floor and move away from the door
go somewhere where i can avoid the draft

Sports car chaperone

At that age when doubt hijacks childhood
sitting sideways in the back of a red sports car
with the top down
and the man whose car it was
who was dating my mother
had gone in to buy cigarettes

and my mother
a small intense serious woman
who did not date often
turned with tears in her eyes and said
*Someday you'll see through me—you'll think one thing
or another, and you'll forgive me or you won't, but
you'll see through me—see me as a person and
not as your mother at all, you may even hate me
for a while.*

I was mystified by the timing
of this exchange
as well as the exchange itself

The man came out tapping a fresh pack of smokes
menthol green

My mother turned her face away
as he climbed into his little car
started the engine and drove

Poor guy, i thought
that cigarette sure smelled good though

The Change

It happened in a week
I was staying at my aunt's
A friend phoned her and i answered
Hello?
Who's this?
Evelyn's nephew.
You can't be Evelyn's nephew—you sound like a girl.
No, really. . .

A few days later
i phoned my father
Hello?
Dad?
Who's this?
Your son.
My son? but my son is still a boy
and you
sound like a man.

I had arrived
somewhere between local
& long distance

His legacy

We couldn't grow vegetables because
people who grew vegetables
in his mind
did so from necessity
We couldn't use the dryer
for the same reason we couldn't turn on the heat
He strung clothes on a line inside the house
because if hung outside
people might think we had no dryer
or worse
that we were poor
I couldn't shower over two minutes
soak, soap, then rinse
I couldn't open the refrigerator without knowing precisely what it
was i was looking for
He had weathered depressionary times
overseas in his plundering naval sinecure
He grew up poor, technically died rich
but he was always poor
far as i was concerned

He was my grandfather
and i hated him then
and i hate him still
He taught me this
This was all he taught me
as well as to turn the light off
whenever i leave the room
which often
i let burn
whether i'm in there
or not

Getting drunk 'round the
sacred relics of my youth

The 18th century porcelain clock
above the scarcely used fire place, its tools & screen
the Steinway seldom played
the stain glass peacock
the ceramic bric-a-brac. . .

The library's
ancient religious tomes
that no one read
Reader's Digest condensed novels
children's books
Churchill's two part history of WW2

these things
this house
her death

This is where i learned the difference
between rich and poor
and this whiskey
this earthy denominator
rendering it absurd

a means to measure
the distance
of my fall

Parade

Your life on a series of floats
Mom and dad atop a shiny '56 convertible
young and smiling

There's you in a bassinet in that small flat in Oxford
Potty-training on a yellow duck
There's the log cabin and the little house in Geyserville
and a dozen goats corralled by your dog, Brownie
forever running, chasing, falling behind

Here comes every girl you ever loved
twirling batons, advancing chronologically
high stepping it, letting their panties show

Behind them a marching band
various pals and others, playing something
familiar and loathsome
you can neither place nor whistle

More floats shadowed by large figurines
sentimental embarrassments that still fly
There's San Francisco and Mill Valley. . .

The Humboldt County float is fun
bunch of stoned long-haired drunkards
partying in the stump of a redwood
trailed by 19 police cars with flashing red lights
There's jail and the bookmobile
and, oh-my-god, here comes theatre. . .

You begin to wish you had brought a chair
or at least a larger flask

Here comes the ex-wives float
And amidst continual confetti and tiresome tickertape

comes Philly, Houston, Chicago, London. . .
The routine begins to feel redundant
like the parade could be vamping for itself
before the float of dead pals & others arrive
You'd remove your hat if you wore one

Following this, your gray-haired mother
alone now in that same convertible of before
both showing their age

And there's your daughter and her expanding brood
future and festering lineage
Your slim stake in a grim tomorrow
They wave and smile from a black and silver SUV
The twirling sperm kites on sticks is a nice touch
and the giant Jesus balloon and happy face says the rest

There's Seattle and wife
present pals and current life
you hop on—still able

A hearse brings up the rear
You stay ahead of it for the time being
How cliché, you think
parades and cliché can't go anywhere
without one another

Not too long a life
but plenty long enough
for a parade

2
Man
about town

At Byron Barous off Clark Street

They asked us to leave
after we'd been drinking there
for some time
and we did
for a little while
until Martin said we should go back in
and moon the bartender
which he did
Too low and half-assed
i said.
Like this, you moron.
I climbed up on a stool
got my pants down, my underwear down
bent over with my ass level to the bar
right where the bastard had to see it
then lost my balance
fell over, stool and all
with my bare ass onto
that ancient peanut shell, dust bunny, tumble weedium
splinter riddled, nail exposed, tar & gum filled cracked bare-board
floor
with its hundred year old filth
trod upon by rebels and convicts and sailors with syph
soldiers on AWOL, slumming frat-boys, drunken Irish—like Martin
and the poets who don't write
and the writers who never say
what they mean

From across the bar i could hear Martin laughing
braying like an asshole
and the bartender
who had missed it all
telling us to leave
all over again
as i struggled to join
my belt and buttons
clutching dignity
from the jaws
of a bad moon rising

Folded

She was a chain-smoking bad tempered drunk
beautiful, Irish, surly
but she could really fold clothes
She worked at the GAP
folded clothes all day
would arrive home
refold whatever i may have folded
and fold that which i had not

We lived on the floor without furniture
Bottles lined the walls
the ashtrays overflowed
There was no dresser or closet
and these folded clothes sat in neat little piles
along the walls
where bottles had not yet been placed

There were more than a few wrinkles in our relationship
but aside from the cigarette burns
our clothes looked good
and the creases for the most part
were where they belonged
making it easy
that last time i packed

Used Furniture

Why's it called skid row?
Because men on the skid gather there.
Don't women go there too?
Not as often as the men.
Will we see dad down there?
Not today.

She drove her new used car
There was plenty of parking in that part of town
The sidewalks lay wide and empty
Papers and wrappers drifted by
Pigeons stood their ground
Bottles and cans lined doorways of places no longer open

Where are all the bums?
Shh, don't call them bums.
Hobos?
Hobos live near freight trains.
Winos?
Shh.
Well, what do i call them?
Don't call them, and don't speak to anyone.

I kept my eye out for whatevertheywerecalled
We went in one of the big cheap furniture stores
A slight man with mustache, wearing a tie and no jacket waited on mom
I looked at a wind-up Victrola

Come on, we're leaving.
Aren't we buying any furniture?
Not here.
Why. . .
Come on.

Back outside i saw a man on the sidewalk
I walked up to him
He wore a hat and when he looked up i saw he had an eye missing
I was going to ask if he were a bum or wino but asked where his eye went?

What? You see it?
He laughed and i saw his eye wasn't all he was missing
Mom yanked me away
I told you not to talk to anyone.

We rounded a corner from the main street
There were 20 to 30 men in the shadows, standing, sitting, waiting
Wow, look at 'em all. What are they waiting for?
I don't know, come on.
She would not let go of me now
We crossed to the empty side
and entered another furniture store
A bald guy with glasses and suspenders waited on mom
She continued to hold my hand
The man was showing her dressers
I felt mom jump then move away from the man

I don't believe this.
What, what?
We left the store
He grabbed my behind.
Is that why we left the other place?
He made an indecent proposal.
What's an indecent proposal?
Nevermind. We're going to Sears. They have to be gentlemen there or
they lose their jobs.
And then what? They end up here?
It would seem, that or in the used furniture business.

We got back to the car
My hand was getting sore
I saw a man across the street pissing in a doorway
I raised an arm to point this out
Mom pushed me in on her side
He turned as we started the car
He smiled wide and slowly put himself away
His teeth were really white and strong
He was all there

Jello shots

My job today is to stand by these cars
smile
pass out flyers
talk to people
4 spanking new cars in the center of the mall
I wear a tie and hold a dust rag
and am still very drunk from the night before

There were jello-shots at this party
Green was vodka
Orange was tequila
normally i don't mix
but it seemed odd to only eat green
or orange
and then there was whatever else there was
beer, pot, whiskey. . .

Each time i smile
i think i might throw up
I wander from car to car
catch dust motes as they land
Nobody gives a shit about these cars
they are not the type to inspire much
They look like half the cars in the parking lot
only cleaner, newer
Nobody wants the brochures i hand them
I collect them from the trash
restack and place them on the car's rear
I notice that these small cars have big trunks
which are also accessible from the back seat
by simply putting down the seat
you can slip into the trunk from inside the car

No one had come to check on me
whenever i wandered into the parking lot
to smoke a bowl
no one took any notice
I climb inside one of the cars and shut the door

then climb in back like i'm checking something
People continue to pass by
they notice the cars just enough
to not bump into them
I bring down the back seat
slip into the trunk and lift the seat back up
just before it clicks
were it to click, i'm not sure if i could get out or not

It is pitch black inside but i can hear the minions
the mallites and mallabies, the human hordes
humming round out there
I get comfortable careful not to rock the delicate
pinion shocks
loosen my tie
listen as bits of conversation wash past

I imagine someone official
suddenly opening the trunk
exposing my bald hangover
my slacker insubordination
It is this fear
an hour or so later
that brings me back
through the seat that didn't quite click
out the passenger door
and more sick now than drunk
back on my feet
wiping my brow with a clean rag
prepared to answer
any automotive question
except for where i've been
or what weight motor oil i've been drinking
I feel particularly knowledgeable
qualified even
to discuss trunk size
and even
show them the boot

Life in bars

We lived in bars
the Irish bars on Clark street
the downtown dives
the good happy hour bargains
the late night early morning piano bars
the bars that stayed open
after all the others had closed
the bars that opened early
featuring a good bloody mary
and signature sausage gravy
the bars with no questions asked
the bars with the best juke box
the bars with bands and no cover
the bars with pitchers and neverending pretzels
and meatballs with toothpicks
bars where i avoided some and sought out others
literary bars and sports bars
bars with steamed hot dogs
and a tv wherever you turned
bars where the bartender told good jokes
daytime bars, old man bars
that all black bar where my Irish sweetie asked
the men playing pool: *talk black to me.*
They bought us drinks the rest of the night
Bars where everyone knew your name
and bars where nobody talked, nobody went to
that only seemed to exist for you

The bar i worked in and met her at and lost my bartender job
for having served her
the bar we could never go back into
after she fell backward on her stool
and i carried her home and put her to bed
before going out
to another bar

The Luckiest man alive

It was some kind of corporate fin de siècle salute to sports
sponsored by ESPN in a mall where i was earning 15 bucks an hour
to stand around and wear a sporty ESPN shirt
talk sports and baby sit the exhibit
which consisted of plaques and pennants and trivia
and a life sized moving talking statue of Lou Gehrig
doing his 'Luckiest man alive,' speech
which he performed in 1939 at Yankee stadium
while dying of his own disease

Would he be known for his 1934 triple crown?
or his consecutive games played
since eclipsed by Cal Ripkin?
No, Lou Gerhig is known for Lou Gerhig's disease
and this was that sad-assed speech where he began
to undermine his legend

I bought a yo-yo which is a more active way of doing nothing
A yo-yo is like doing nothing with an exclamation point attached

Kids lurked everywhere, ready to steal Lou's cap
drop his pants
humiliate the luckiest man on earth
anyway they could

I walk the dog
zip round the world
become semi-proficient with my blue yo-yo
listen as Lou says the words over and over
*Today, today, I consider myself, myself, the luckiest man, man, alive,
alive. . .*
I think about how much luckier Babe Ruth was
he chased pussy instead of being one
7 decades later Lou is still a big corporate sponsored pussy

I have five years on him already
with no idea what to do with my life
playing with a blue yo-yo in a brightly lit mall
and no disease to call my own

This kind of work

leaves the hands hard
the mind soft
all day
day after day
it takes its toll
on the ears
the back
your knees
the arches in your feet

The kind of work
you can wear the same shirt
2 days in a row
don't need to shave or
clean your nails
drilling, pounding, lifting
measuring
exactness
inserting something in something
to code
to specifications
as other eyes inspect
Rampant curses
sonic boom belching
the hollow slam of a plastic door
to the latrine
The check in the mail
already spent

The kind of work
they warned you of
if you didn't do what they said

and you didn't
and now you do

Progress

On our walks around the city
this girl i used to date
would recall
what went where:

That used to be a dog kennel.
That was once a record store.
Over there used to be a Thai-restaurant.

I wasn't as fascinated by the history
as with her ability to remember
She was still in her 20's
but her recall was that
of an ancient elephant

I thought of her just today
seeing a fresh empty lot
something just destroyed
its pieces piled up in a green dumpster
erased from the corner and ready
for the next thing

Last week something stood there
I had walked by it as i walked by now
Whatever it had been was already lost to me

Whatsherface would have remembered

Appetizer

Pam and i are at the pizza parlor waiting
for #37 and
i am looking at people
Everyone is a little pasty and overweight
as though they'd been on pizza
all their lives
There are several families assembled
who fit this description as well as being
descriptively nondescript
Fueled by Frescas and coke, the youngsters
pop up and down like toast
with more quarters from dad
drawn magnetically to video games
ZURP ZOOM ZIP ZAP and ZO on
world war 3-4-5 ad infinitum are
waged with renewed vigor
A man with the crack of his ass smiling over
and no quarters
loiters around the kids
He is the kind of man that makes me glad
i have no children
In walks another man and 2 women
who buy beer and
build a salad to the sky
The man wears a beard, glasses, and a cap like Chico Marx
I've seen him before at bars finishing drinks
others have left behind
They order more beer and all of them eat the overflowing salad
He smokes while eating and
his leg jerks up and down beneath the table like a dog's
A fat kid in a baseball uniform sponsored by Barnes Drugs
keeps roaring past from pizza to ww3 and
back again
He is the most relentless panhandler i have ever seen
(in at least the past hour)
His twice as big, twice as fat father
keeps shelling it out and eating pizza
It is quite obvious he no longer cares

about anything
His equally fat wife's jowls quiver and shake
as she keeps stuffing it in and
washing it back with diet coke
The pedophile keeps leaning over the lost boys
One of the women sitting with the bearded Chico
has melon sized tits
She wears no bra, talks animatedly
her tits undulate all over the table
She too doesn't care
Pam—sitting judiciously with her back to all this
stares into the rising bubbles of our pitcher—
asks—*what are you looking at?*
Nothing i say.
#37 is called
and i get up

French quarter, Fat Tuesday, 2009

The streets were filthy with beads, piss, beer, puke
a week of debauchery fallen in a single day
with drunks of every nationality, race, class
unified, surrendering and slumming with the bottle
buttloads of bottles, cans
and those ubiquitous bright green plastic grenades
called the Hurricane, manufactured husks and human husks
littered the streets, filled the sidewalks

A plump girl in a tight purple dress and heels ran past us
pursued by a greasy young man, lanky, dark, unctuous, a mustache
looked like he pumped gas for a living
She was blond, made up, pissed off
stopped beside the building before us
She had been crying
He grabbed her, tried to kiss her
She clocked him
They fell back into a doorway of a business not open

A half block later
she ran by again and again he followed
her ass straining through that purple dress
stretched like a second skin
her fleshy shoulders, heaving with emotion, heavy with anger
He grabbed her, she swung at him
He blocked this, held her wrist
She sobbed into the crook of his neck
He stroked her curly dyed blond hair
Her eyes bled darkness all over him

The streets were full of staggering beaded people
some costumed and masked
trying to be with it, have a good time, score
Or a good time gone bad, trying to get out of it
get loose, stay tight, not fall, not get beamed by beads from above
or, in our case, rear-ended from behind
as again she raced by

and again he caught up
shook her like you should never shake a baby
She broke his hold, her metal fists opened like flowers
her painted nails, spread, clutched the air
His were extended, stained, pleading
It looked like the end of something or a brand new war torn
beginning
Not a comedy that's for sure
—*Last Tango in French Quarter*—
I could already hear the music
minor keys, somber base, tortured brass

She passed us again, heels under her arm
her fishnet feet black from the street
everything pulling within that tight hemline
that big round purple ass moving like a planet
orbiting our gravity
They formed a single silhouette
He into her and she into him
Swallowed by the night

Just another couple on fat tuesday
too much something, maybe one another, maybe something else
full of rage, hurt, hormones, youth, too-much-to-drink, you name it
these kids had it all

Oh, to be in love like that again

The Interns

The boys were all gay
and the girls just wanted to be taken seriously
but sometimes i got lucky anyway
We studied Shakespeare and Chekhov
speech and dance and voice and movement
Mostly we moved furniture, built sets, carried spears
and occasionally got a line or two
My roommate, David, sucking back a smoke
The bathhouses, you have no idea. . .
And he and the others would go
as i practiced drinking alone
praying for a war or at least a cause
listening to the next Glen Close or Meryl Streep
crying into the phone that she was ready

I would survive these one & two night stands
these one & two year relationships
In time i would do all those jobs we
at 19, 20, 21 & 22
thought beneath us
I learned that acting was not an art form
or even much of a craft
but an endurance marathon
a combination of luck and charm and perseverance
a precarious balance between the creation of your myth
and survival of your legend

Whenever i go to the movies or watch t.v.
i pay close attention to the credits
I keep looking for them
hoping somebody might have made it
become what we all wanted
instead of taking that fast fade into that crowded constellation
where everybody looks the same
while some of us
are still around
to watch

The Buffer Zone

Excuse me for my boorish behavior
but your behavior bores me
It's not your fault
nor mine
just the way it sways n staggers
as the case served cold
stands
within this frosty condescension
problematic i fear. . .
Hell, i can't even explain
without another beer
It aint like i can't face my problems
it's that your problems
or, rather
the problem of you
has me faced
That host of mortal woes
you shroud yourself in
that you share with any and all
has me reaching for the shelf
And it's not you in particular
it is you en masse
that whole messy populated mass
to whom i've built my alcoholic fortress
my cannabis sativa citadel
where i alone may dwell
within these nicotined stained walls and windows
seeing the world
through soft amber glass
at a distance

Vaudevillian wedding

Under the big top billowing yellow and white
with straw
don't forget the straw
where elephants go
or in this case dogs
Essence of dog permeating rancorous
The calliope cranks up
as do the fires
Nothing to eat but shell fish and cake
Clams grip our guts as oysters lay still born in the coals
shut tight as a pawn shop on Yom Kipper
Another sleight of hand artist offering extended shrift
A glass harmoniums haunting refrain
A comedian filling air
Do you promise to appear, obey, delay. . .
Garbage piled high
and stuff
much other stuff
rivaling nature
always rivaling nature
because that is the nature of stuff
old dryers, tubs, fridges. . .
you know—stuff
And the dogs lap at the flames
they don't care if its not the month for oysters
Chubby teens twirl and dance
as aged hippies smoke and grin
remembering something perhaps forgotten
I now pronounce you. . .
for as Mark Twain once said—You can kiss my ass
though he may have plagiarized it
And we feed in the dark like wolves without their discipline
as the dogs dog us into the night
and onto the morrow
when we pull the slugs up from the carpet
pack up our tents and go home

Taunting the tiger

Because they know nothing of nature
it
or their own
from their own zoo
they enter this one
Three fools on Christmas day
probably with new sweaters on
nursing the glow of vodka and pot

Bengal, bagel, they don't care
They taunt, they tease
they could be at a strip club
or torturing the women in their lives
while *it* paces, narrows its yellow eyes

Kipling had it right
Shere Khan does indeed hate mankind
and would hate these young men
even without cause

The young men move on
young, numb, dumb, cruel
they have never been prey
they have never been vulnerable that way
unthinkable, forgotten already
not one iota of concern that their bravado
could return to bite them in the ass

Targeting the one with the biggest mouth
no endangered species he
getting him right by the exit
like preordained irony
like god really could be keeping score

Great hunters sometimes kill for no reason but this wasn't one of them
yet they killed that tiger for no good reason
they called it something else but killed it all the same

They should have given that tiger a medal

Based on a true story, San Francisco Zoo, San Francisco, Christmas, 2007.

Vote

I go to vote
I am but a bit of sand
sifted from one vast pan
to the next
depending on which poll you read
I have pieces of paper in hand
reminding me who i'm for

Old ladies at a long table
or were they long ladies at an old table
ask my name
give me a ballot
send me to a booth
I place the card in the slot and
begin punching holes

I finish up in the booth
check my fly upon exiting
with my little punched card placed in an envelope
to preserve my anonymity from having punched
CERTAIN holes versus
others and hand it
to one of the long ladies
like a vial of blood
to their aged smiles

Later
everything i voted for
lost
Guess i must have punched
all the right holes

At the bus stop in passing

Six or more stood waiting for the bus
watching him, looking at her
If i was a young man. . . said the old man to a young girl
Her back was to me, leaning against a building
i'm an old fuck, i'm 64. . .
but if i were a young man. . .

He stood apart from the others
more drunk than old
I'd. . .
His voice was hideous
but his face was silky smooth
like he had carefully shaved that morning
before getting hammered
while the streets filled up with those
trying to get home

I slowed down wanting to hear what he would indeed do
were he a young man and not an old fuck, at 64

She was blonde and lovely and possibly only 12 years old
but probably older than that
with an easy Mona Lisa detachment to counter this old fuck's odd
declarative
an apparent compliment he felt compelled to make
An older gal would not have stood his stale bravado
with such innocent panache

I couldn't walk any slower without stopping
hoping he would make his point
all talk and out of liquor too
As young as she was she looked
like she'd been lied to before

I thought about her afterward
while looking at old paintings
at the Frye Museum
I didn't think much of him
at all

50

She said

—I never thought i'd see the day
when i'd be reduced to a poem
 I said
—I haven't reduced anything
If
anything
i've expanded your immortality
 She said
—You're full of shit

Hi Honey

welcome home
I was going to do the dishes
but i couldn't find the sponge
I was going to take out the trash
but we're out of bags
I would've swept and vacuumed
but there was too much crap on the floor
and on the table and dresser
and i couldn't find a rag to dust
and you know there's no point in doing the floors
if you don't dust first
I did gather up all the beer cans and wine bottles
but the truck was broken down
so i couldn't take them to the recycling center
so i stuck them in your closet instead
And i'm sorry about the bathroom
The toilet really wasn't my fault
and i don't know what the cat did in the tub
but i guess her cat box was full
and you know i can't do that job without puking
I did put clean sheets on the bed
You should have seen me here without you
I lived like hell
It's good to have you home

Sunbathing

They were sitting there
talking
or rather, she was talking
he was trying to read

She said
I hate the sun
I wish it were hot without the sun.

Go to Houston, he said
worse place i ever lived.

The shade was moving in
He slid over to stay in the sun
She stayed where she was
letting the shadow over take her
as the gulf between them
grew

Ode to my dental hygienist

She flashes her hygienic smile
asks how i've been, changes
in my health? The conversation
quickly turns to teeth, mine

Good, she says, x-rays next time
but today just a basic cleaning
She adjusts my chair, adjust herself
around that chair, places her near
flat chest beside my face with a cord
she runs up under my arm
I open. I am hers and i turn
and pivot at her touch, she, who could
bring me to my knees were i not already
on my back. The whirring begins, the
scrapping & digging isn't bad but the tiny
spinning, whirling needle, like a miniature
jackhammer, enters my brain, raising
the thumbs of my once resting hands
as i try not to think of that Marathon Man movie
when Larry Olivier asks Dustin Hoffman, *Is it safe?*

I trust my sweet dental technician and remain
hers, opening wide, accommodating and anticipating
her every command, sneaking peeks at her through my
cheap spattered sunglasses, while my tongue
stands in the middle of my mouth like an
awkward party guest and my lips crack
like old china while my saliva glands attempt to
make sense of the whole. This girl half my age
and earning three times my annual salary
can hurt me like no one else as i am her's for
a full hour, until four months from now when i
am hers again. She tells me things with her hands
in my mouth. Words collect in my brain before
they vanish from lack of voice. She will never know
my feelings for her, this intimacy like no other, without teeth

While you were gone
i slept on your side of the bed
i climbed the stairs backward
i stood on the porch and howled at an absent moon
with your panties on
the red ones which i then
put neatly away
Bottles clustered like bowling pins
dishes piled like buildings
i take them down with terrorist finesse
a perfect strike

I kept the ball-peen hammer in the freezer
i chased squirrels from the yard
i consulted runes
rued the result
i scared ghosts from our pantry
got drunk three times and
cried 17
ate blackeye peas and gruel and bratwurst with honey mustard
i thought 72 immoral and lewd unlawful acts
committing several without even trying
i masturbated using only my left hand
i bathed in mayonnaise
i found your diary and your dildo
i couldn't help myself
i read your dildo
but i did not insert your diary
some things cannot be

Funny
with you gone
i feel i know you better
than when you are here

Hurry back
I know too much about you already

Finding it

It's a daily occurrence
whenever i can't find something
i must ask for it
out loud even
to the woman i live with

Where's the sponge?
Where are my keys?
Have you seen the. . .
or my stash, or my flask, or
just about anything
within this vast lexicon
of misplaceable items

I can look for an eternity
but until i give voice to my hunt
i never find what i'm looking for

Having asked however
i locate it immediately

She doesn't tell me where it is
she doesn't know any better than i do
it is enough to have asked
it works every time

I don't know what i did before her
but i'm glad she's here to help me find things
and that i found her
and that between us
this slim magic
continues

Tomatoes

It was a good year for tomatoes
cherries and beefeaters
green vines inching here and there
appearing overnight even
topped with little yellow flowers

I liked smelling my fingers
after picking them
hundreds, perhaps thousands. . .

It was a bad year for Iraq
Afghanistan, the Cubs, Rush Limbaugh, Saddam Hussein
rain forests, polar icecaps, the great barrier reef
Africa

It was a good year for fires
and mud slides
and presidential pals and cronies

And the votes still out on us
her and i
but we were better off for the tomatoes

And as the weather worsened
and those green on the vine
failed to ripen
blackened and fell
we still had sauce and had dried a bunch
and some few remained
miraculously fresh and eatable and sweet
thick skin and all

And the soil next year would be spent
and it was still too soon to know
whether the same might be said for us
but at least we had them
those beautiful sweet red tomatoes
goddammit but they were good

The Day the Kingdome came down

i got us up early. Packed a flask, a pipe, beers. . .
Brush your teeth, your hair, let's go, i said.

We walked the same several miles, i had
traveled many times, finding a grassy
knoll with a good view of the Kingdome
overlooking I-5, weirdly still and empty, shut
down for today's demolition. We milled about
like at a rock concert with bad seats. There
was the Smith Tower alongside other towers
whose decks and porches teamed with people
Ferries cut cross the Sound
Everything looked as it usually did, as we waited
gazing at this concrete pimple, designed to last
as long as time, or the Pyramids, or baseball itself
just twenty four years old and sentenced to death
We watched and studied this massive condemned tit
in its final hour
They couldn't really be taking it down, could they?

There'd been some good seasons, some great games
Regardless of how the M's were doing, there was
many a night i'd say to myself, for five bucks, you can
see Ken Griffey Jr., Alex Rodriguez, Edgar Martinez
maybe Randy Johnson, and for better or worse, the Mariner Moose

There was that unfortunate time, i was arrested, smoking
pot in the concourse. I listened to the rest of the game
from a small barred cell in the bowels of the dome
The M's who had been down 4 to 1 came back to win without me
Muffled cheers seeped down through the bars
where i listened like a gladiator about to go on
Another happier game, i caught not one but two foul balls
leaning out from the middle tier, giving my second
to a small child, whose father flinched in fear

It was a horrible place for baseball. Sounds reverberated

off the artificial turf. The air felt stagnant, everything echoed
The Big Unit pitched impressively but mostly the ball just
sailed out, everyone hit homers if they hit anything at all

On the day the Kingdome came down, it was dry and clear
baseball season had yet to begin. A helicopter passed over
breaking the stillness. Someone stood. Someone else stood
I stood, she stood, we all stood, like the National Anthem
were about to be sung. We gazed at this monstrosity
with its exoskeletal walkways. The flag, i noticed
no longer flapped from above

Red rays raced out from the spokes to the outer rim
The earth rumbled. The nipple, where the flag used to be
began to sink. It fell like a giant soufflé. A great roar preceded
billows of gray white dust, hiding that which fell. Fragmenting
chunks caved as dust bloomed, burying several thousand baseball
games, a hundred or more football games, car shows, Monster truck
rallies, home, garden & boat shows, political events. . . gone and
buried
in the time it took to round the bases

And you can tell it goodbye. . .

We cheered, we cheered like the M's had just come from behind
Like Edgar had hit another game winning double
We cheered from our hilly vantage, as a vast gust of dust plumed
over us, blotting out the sky, expanding like a cancer that might
consume us all. Cheers and screams trailed all over town
I nipped some scotch and squeezed my woman close beside me
because we wouldn't be around to see our own deaths, or even
one another's and even if we did, it could never equal what we
had just seen—this huge forever thing, no longer there

Last day on earth

On this the last day on earth
i bathe, wash my hair, clean my nails
shave with a new blade

I dress because there's a chill in the air
put on that nice silky Hawaiian shirt
Make coffee and use my favorite mug
Van Gogh *Starry nights* the one with the little chip on the lip

I do all the things i normally do
try and pay attention to each task
without thinking, gee, i won't be doing this anymore
That could drive me crazy before this day is done

I'd spend even more time staring out the window
and looking at the sky than usual
I'd gaze at my car from the porch
It will be crazy on the roads today

With my third cup of coffee i add a shot
finishing that single malt i'd been saving
I smoke that bud i've had around for a while too
Then perhaps eat that Viagra someone gave me that i've had forever
but was afraid of
that: *erection over four hours see your physician. . .* warning
I could never tell if that was for real or just advertising?
anyway, what can i lose today?

I'd make love to my wife
I'd try and take my time
but probably wouldn't exceed four hours
With the time left over i'd spread out all my favorite porn mags
and hold a contest as to my very favorite

I'd already have made us a nice breakfast
with my special crispy potatoes and perfect overeasy eggs

and we'd eat them on the porch
along with a tall bloody mary
while listening to Frank Sinatra
and perhaps dance a couple turns
I'd probably want to write a poem
but would resist this impulse

We'd talk of course but it'd be a vastly different kind of discussion
None of that, when are you going to get a job kind of stuff
or could you clean out the garage, or is tonight recycling?
or the house sure is getting dirty kind of talk
We wouldn't discuss 'the relationship'
We'd be on to more personal metaphysical digressions
during which i'd probably make another cocktail
while she clutched the cat and we'd both cry and maybe she'd
get her guitar and play that song she's never really played for me

She'd want to call her mother
and i'd want to check emails and open one last day of mail
but nothing would have come and it wouldn't matter if it did
And i'd pull her off the phone, smash it
beside where i had already smashed the clock and television
And we'd discuss how we should have gotten together with so and
so
one last time, deciding it would have been too painful
on this the last day

We'd continue, sitting together
taking turns holding the cat, holding each other
sharing bits of conversation, listening to our
favorite tunes and discussing what to do for dinner
and I'd go make us martinis instead with lots of olives
while our eyes continued trained on the sky
watching it get dark
waiting for the end together
waiting for it both alone

3
Nature & natural crimes

The Frenzy of the red berry

They appear en masse like some outlaw biker gang
descending like locusts, raining like toads, pelting the earth
like children spilling into the playground, drunk and tumbling
pie-eyed into the 2 a.m. dawn, racing full throttle around the yard,
swooping then flashing
in rust colored autumnal solidarity
Swoosh swoosh, they dive, their wings beat frantic like all existence
hinged on it

Beating one another out as if embroiled in multidimensional chess
without deliberation, like Huns chasing down the Sabine Women,
screaming shrieking aerial dynamos, daredevils, hot-dogging
hotshots, rebels without a pause
Engaged in some cosmic carte blanche ribbon cutting all-you-can-eat
heat

Orbs of red clusters, vulnerable as testicles, bright like lanterns
beacons of temptation, picking them off in their yellow beaks
gorging greedily, ripping at 'em like Promethean entrails, stealing
and
resting their feathered corpulence on bobbing branches, hearts rapid-
fire,
pitter-patter swallowing as they seize another and another, more and
more

They are everywhere in a flash—20, 30. . .
hurtling and Hitchcockian, spinning, twirling like spastic lariats
dashing dipsomaniacal, magically avoiding collision
without yielding one feather of cartwheeling cock-surety

Four robins, i imagine to be the senior sages
splash, giddy and gaga in the concrete birdbath
the anchor of this hub
Wiser perhaps, fatter it seems, more mature, possibly, they vie for
perspective
like old men with little hard-ons they cheer the youngsters on
splash and wade with uncontained zeal. The flurry of

berrymania, berrypalooza, berryphilia, filled with an insatiable
gluttonous crimson fed, narcotic-fused, feather-stuffed, bird-bracing
ecstasy
These seniors shake their heads, pump their birdy fists, catch their
reflective colors
splash with glee and rejuvenating joy, dip, flap, flutter, lowering their
bright plump bellies, displacing the brackish water, shake the wet
from their wings
before rejoining the youngsters
Join or Die, and maybe join then die
in between which—fly fly. . .

And then it is over
as instantaneous as it began, as if some secret alarm had sounded
and they take to the greater elsewhere, the big blue, beating passage
returning the scene back to the calm that prevails
as the yard settles
beneath the yellowing maple and its stripped bare branches
its nearly fallen leaves, spinning twirling seeds, concluding
with bunches of untapped berry clusters
left behind like random booty from an interrupted robbery

The air reverberates with their departure
like a battlefield after, only no where near as sad
as a big sleepy orange tabby crawls out from under somewhere

This brave voyeur saunters out, watchful cautious, travels the seed
laden lawn, the crab grass, moss, clover, twigs, scattered berry husks
shell-shocked worms, nervous beetles. . .
leaps up upon the birdbath, sniffs the tainted water
does not drink
gazes philosophically into the sky
blinks
then continues on, disappearing slowly
into the dying azaleas and fallen foxglove

Black dog

You can tell when the black dog is home
The bed goes unmade
The letters don't get writ
that which arrives is junk
The ringing phone, an accident
It's the black dog calling from somewhere
bow wow wowing on a wire
dogging them on
It's the worse feeling i know
this feeling of no feeling
that feeling that all feeling's fled
Thoughts don't conclude
sentences go unfinished
there wasn't anything to say anyway
and no one to say it to
The black dog is here
howling at an eclipsed moon
There is nothing to eat
nothing to smoke
nada to drink
that'll chase him away
Steady as a pug
tenacious as a pit
the black dog remains
lifting its leg on all you hold dear
He remains
faithful
'til finally
you bare your teeth
scare him off
knowing it is one or the both of you
and regardless
he'll be back

Sheep

Only a century ago
we lived half as long
You were lucky maybe
to survive long enough
to get cancer
have a heart attack
go mad
A splinter could kill you
measles, polio, yellow fever
a wayward horse
a cold
People were tougher
but only because the weak
did not last

These days they run things
stationed in cubicles
climate controlled florescent domiciles
with arch and back and wrist support
psychic support, grief counseling
swarm mentality
weaklings banding together
to discuss what they perceive
holds power
unions and agencies and departments
designed to protect them
lawyers who fight their fights for them
vicariously living through sports
war, politics, celebrity plightfalls
making children
making the world safe
for more pussies
with greater ever escalating fear
as they keep their heads low
graze and face
the same direction
upwind
from the slaughter house

Chickens

There are roughly as many chickens as humans
People consume one million chickens a minute
Every minute, world wide, there are 245 human births
versus 102 deaths

I try and do the math but cannot *

Will we have 7 billion chickens in another couple of years?
Will we have ten to fifteen billion chickens by mid century?
Will there be room for anything other than chickens and people?
And what about cows?

There are not enough tree climbing primates
as of this writing, to fill a small sports stadium

A thousand of this, a few hundred of that. . .
down to a dozen. . . poof
gone like an unpaid magicain's assistant

Things go extinct all the time,
sez Rush Limbaugh
it's a natural progression.

Just us
and the chickens
cockroaches. . .
flies, maggots. . .
blackberries
Rush Limbaugh
& death
do-dah, do-dah. . .

*83 million new people per year.

Apology to the frogs

The biggest die-off
in 80 million years
comes not from space
has not been smote by god
or from overhunting
or because we covet your hide
or tusks

The French think you're good to eat
but then they also find
Jerry Lewis funny

Like the canary in a coal mine
you are the harbinger of doom

but more studies are needed
it's a natural cycle
survival of the fittest
a dog-screw-dog kind of planet

As the geniuses of commerce and industry
scowl at their screens
monitoring their purported wealth
you *ribbitt*
and *needeep*
and croak
in tainted meadows
dried-up wetlands
new housing projects and future malls
i apologize
with the same bottomed-out guilt
the drunken driver feels
convicted of vehicular homicide

sorry for my victim
sorry i got caught
sorry mister toad's wild ride is over

Bison

We nearly succeeded
in killing them off
Not the brightest of beasts
socially adept, bad eyesight
stampedes easily
ready to race off a cliff
or into a ravine
with its head as hard as a hood ornament
an ass barely in attendance
They like to rut and butt
romp and stomp and roam
saunter briskly through flower filled fields

Too lean of meat for caucasians
but all essential for the Indian
back when the west was being won
as so much was increasingly lost

Here in Yellowstone, where these beasts
are no smarter than anywhere else
they have no memory
of what a gun blast can do
and have lost their fear of us, and
ordinarily that is not good
but for now

it doesn't matter
as they click and clack
across the asphalt
holding up
all the smiling traffic
it's more than okay
as we fire away
getting one after another
with our digital cameras

this creature once so common
we have come so far to see

Cancer protocol

Did not send cards
Did not make phone calls
the call to my mother
was more than enough

The throat
therein lies the goat
when ever i whisper its name
he jabs a horn into
its soft red wall

It's the mother
of all sore throats
Can't drink or smoke
to make it better

back to you
sorry
there was no good way to say it
no rosy light to shine
no spin to lessen how it might land

You will see me when i'm better
or figure, no news is more of the same

Despite any appearance to the contrary
you will tell me how good i'm looking
and i will catch the next reflection i see
to help determine the size of your lie

Afghan girl

They finally found you
after 17 years
You were surprised
your picture had created any interest
it was good, you said, if it had served
as an inspiration to others
though you expressed mostly shame
with regards to your tattered cloak
you wear such a fine purple burka now

When that same photographer found you
you could only look at his lens
Those once fiery eyes
no longer held any spark
they had grown blunt and stupid

So, you can write your name and recite
several passages from the Koran
lucky you

After 17 years
no one could have hoped to have found that green eyed girl
that wild-eyed orphan with so much hate and passion
I could have loved that girl
but this woman
this dull metamorphosis
mother of two
with a couple of goats and a vegetable patch
and a husband who drained the gold from those sea-green eyes. . .
well, you're as haggard as your country now
born unto your fate
perhaps as it was written
despite that moment
when the National Geographic guy
captured something
dangerous and true
fierce, beautiful
fleeting

Boredom

God got bored and invented man
Man got bored and craved woman
Woman got bored and had kids
One kid got bored and killed the other
And they were off
only god knew where
and even he wasn't sure
He tried to command them
He tried flushing them out
He tried educating them
His boy was killed
And god died soon after
cosmologically speaking
as recorded by philosophers
the iconoclasts
the truly bored

And humanity grew bored
and waged war
grew bored with war
and waged peace
until this grew
too boring
And out of this
all this boring war and peace
television was born
unleashing
boredom
unfathomable

Somewhere on another planet
they are watching I Love Lucy
Gilligan's Beaver
and Walter Cronkite
telling how many died that day
alongside a laughtrack

Cash Cab is coming

The Fallguy

Don't blame god
it wasn't Her fault
it had nuthin' to do with right or wrong
good or evil, you or me, what we said
or didn't say
or how we pray
nothing to do with faith
karma, moral comeuppance, sin
or who was supposed to win

God doesn't look like anyone we know
not Charlton Heston or Brad Pitt
or even Victor Mature
He doesn't sound like James Earl Jones or Ceil B deMille
He never talks to presidents

He doesn't have a favorite town
Mecca, Vegas, Saint Augustine, Katmandu. . .
it's all one to. . .
Doesn't have a sex or even have sex
doesn't have balls or a dick or a cunt or tits or even an ass
doesn't require sugar coated euphemisms
adapts handily to any pronoun—allah them

Doesn't have a favorite team, candidate or party
Doesn't choose anybody over anybody else
one country under. . .
No trust in any currency
Does not control weather
Does not rain on anyone's parade
nor strike lightning when pissed

Gives talent to none
Aristotle, Beethoven or Ricky Henderson. . .
God doesn't give one goddamn about any of it
Does not take offense when cursed
Does not answer mail
Will not return calls

Across the universe, you aint nothin' but a hound dog

Elvis learned to sing the devil's music in church
he was bigger than Jesus, but he would never have said it
John Lennon was in awe, called their brief encounter
the greatest single night in his then still young career

What if Colonel Parker had traded places with Brian Epstien?
The Beatles would never have lost those stupid suits
Would their hair have evolved?
Imagine all those silly movies, i wonder if you can
John dancing with Ann Magaret, Paul racing in the Grand Prix
George shakin' his hips, tryin' to look like James Dean
Ringo, wearin a cowboy hat, fist fightin' in a bar. . .

The Fab Four winding it down on the Vegas strip
fat, corporate, landlocked with Sinatra
Rendering The Monkees redundant, the Rolling Stones an obscure
blues band
the British invasion giving way to Memphis

Meanwhile Brian Epstien would have fallen in love with Elvis
They might have swapped hair gel, or else the big E would have let
his face grow long

The Colonel would never have allowed Sargent Peppers
or Yoko Ono, naked album covers, Number 9. . . or
Whata Shame Mary Jane had a Pain at the Party. . .

Having served their stint in the army, the Beatles stumble sleepless
amped up on karate and nebutal, wearing shades, sideburns, lycra
and leather
zippers & sequins & rhinestones, embracing Nixon
helping out as self appointed drug czars, creating fashion mayhem

Elvis and the Maharishi get on surprisingly well
The Maharishi moves to Graceland while Elvis remains in India
performing at the Taj Mahal with his son-in-law Michael
performing duets: Suspicious Minds, Billie Jean. . . and an odd
rendition of
She Came in Through the Bathroom Window & Mean Mister
Mustard
something Elvis visualized on acid, with a gospel country flair

Pop dreams

In my dream i am kicking Justin Bieber's ass
I'd sooner dream i was fucking Angelina Jolie
but kicking Justin Beiber's ass is not without its joy
I smack him in his pretty upturned nose
send a left into those perfect pearly choppers
Course, he's not grinnin' in my dream
he's in tears and flails his thin girly arms
protectively over his flouncy hair
Fans of his stand on the sidelines of my dream
expressing horror at what a prick i am

Yeah, i'd much rather be havin' that other dream
Angelina or that girl who tends bar at the Elysian
Why can't we pick our dreams?
The unfairness of it irks me and
i pass this on into the teen throb's solar plexus
I have nothing against young Bieber
aside from his overly exposed face and his
senseless saccharine pop rock sound—whatever that be
He's merely the IT boy, last year this could have been
Zac Efron, or generational eons ago, Bobby Sherman
who begat David Cassidy, who begat. . .
well, who the fuck cares?
Who the fuck cares, Justin?
I holler. His fans and posse murmur, 'we do, we love Ju. . .'
I silence them with another kick, a low one, as he's on the ground
—and i'm not getting any younger, even in my dreams—

God, what an asshole i am, i pause to watch
as he spits out a couple of teeth
I quickly recover from this bout of self reflection
and kick him again, feeling his ribs give way against my foot
He'll have other problems later but i'm his problem now
Yeah, i'd much rather be fucking Angelina Jolie
but this is what i get instead
IS IT ANY REASON WHY I'M BITTER, JUSTIN?
I give him another, TAKE THAT, i scream in my dream
Both of us hoping one of us wakes up soon

Eating pussy

I've been down here for an hour
licking
sucking
darting my tongue
one way
then the other
round the old pink

My lips have gone numb
the tongue feels ready
to fall off

It's been too long
with too much work
to admit defeat
besides
she's close
writhing
back arched
nipples hard

I've got my hand under there
and am tempted to shove a finger
up something
just to keep myself engaged

I hump the side of the bed
I think about shopping at Safeway
about that funny noise my car's been making
about a poem i might write
if i ever finish up here

I am drowning in her juice
I want to clear my throat
but that would only remind her
that i'm here, too

I wonder what she's thinking of:
the Oakland Raiders
a thousand bikers roaring down the highway
her parent's great dane

Fuck, i have a cramp in my foot
My dick's been going up and down like the stock market
She groans
I groan
I glide my fingers up those lubricaceous holes and halls
She grabs the back of my head
I'm goin' down like alice in cunnilingusland
She jerks with the spasms of the dying
I think i'm going to sneeze

—Oh god, that was great, she says

I clear my throat
scratch my head
wipe my face
rub my foot

My turn

The Fourth rate third reich's second chance at first place

Think what you will
say what you like
but Hermann Goring
the obese world war one ace
drug addict art collector
who garishly costumed himself
like the reich's own Oscar Wilde
at least married well

Frau Goring had many Jewish friends
who through her dubious husband's influence
pipe lined as many if not more
than Schindler
ever listed

She got them out of the country
and Hermann stole their art

Any man who loves Goya
can't be all bad
And a man with a cyanide tooth
who will cheat the judge and jury
and hangman
has my personal respect
however little
that's worth

Space junk

We are on Pluto where the sun is small
We are white holes
exuding light
taking nothing in
We are battered scarred lunar scapes
pocked by past excess
We are seemingly intelligent beings
from different planets
We've studied one another's history
while making allowances for our own
We've too much in common
to want to inhabit the same solar system
much less the same world
We are lost moons orbiting
all past fears and failures
and those voyages
which yielded nothing but stories
lots of stories
which we keep telling
to fill the atmosphere
as our natural resources dwindle
There are things we can never say to each other
it would not translate
We are expanding at hyper white light speed
stretching beyond our comprehension
until all i understand
is my white dwarf is hot for your red giant
i want to rest my mars
within your venus
i want to have my milky way with you
and lap at your molten sun swept shores
reeling you in by lariat
recovering the immense vastness
of this unfathomably colossus cosmos
where we may yet
establish
intelligent life

Pictures of my grandmothers

I have a framed portrait of my mother's mother on the wall
above my desk
It is a glamorized painting, circa 1938
She looks like the Gibson girl from that period earlier
She died when my mother was 14

My father's mother is in an antique frame atop my book case
She is smiling with crooked teeth—1931
She is young in the photo and died not long after
Neither women knew one another
and neither knew me
They would not have known their own children grown up
let alone their only children's only child
Both had sisters—my great aunts, whom i did know
These sisters outlived my grandmothers by many years
They got old and hunched and bald and crippled
They would send me Christmas cards with 20 dollars every year
They have since joined their sisters

I would like to have known my grandmothers
but could not have known them in their prime
as they appear on the wall or bookcase
And they could not have known me in mine
unless it were as a baby
during which
a baby and a doting grandmother
may hit it off
amazingly well

The Nascent stages

You would never have come into being
had it not been for your mother's ass
It spoke to me
in language i was fluent in

She wore a tight brown dress
We stood by a keg, i filled her cup
I was 18, she 17
I was less enthralled once
our mouths had joined
the conversation

We didn't make it that night
but maybe the next
We never dated
I thought she was an idiot
but i wasn't chasing
intellectual stimulation

During our brief affair
we made it on a friend's floor
—a slight deviation from the usual
pressed inside the front seat of my Ford—
Old Town, Eureka, in a building
no longer there

I climaxed just as i heard a train whistle
A huge blast. Dust bunnies were dancing
beneath the bed we for some reason were not on
It was a long whistle
maybe something was on the tracks
but whatever was going on out there
i'm certain
this was the moment

You were on your way

and that train wasn't going to stop
for anything

Problematic prodigy

There are all these things he can work that i can't:
the vcr, dvd, the pc, even the garage door
He just can't seem to keep
the hot chocolate with the tiny marshmallows
from spilling all over the fucking place

12/9/72

That could have been it
Finger on trigger
ready to puke pills with that last hit of vodka
living up to my prognosis
Ready to run
barely able to walk
The semi-automatic in the priest's face
his wife's horror
comical
Their daughter safe
not there
My young partner
some few years shy of his own end
reining me in
loaded like the gun
safeties off

It could have been much worse
like that which makes you shake your head
It all could have ended there
another stat
another burden to the state
tragic insignificance
common as heartbreak

Deserving that beating by the cops
the 6 months in boy's camp
and the sharp flick of the towel
in the showers

The formative years

Boots

I lace 'em up for the umpteenth thousandth time
My mother bought me these
when i was 16 and had just been sentenced to a work farm
which she was none too pleased
with me for getting sent there
I was marching off to hell
but i would go in sound footwear

They are covered in scars
the once black toes are just raw leather
evidence of a chainsaw
that almost made it through

I revere these boots
I wonder what the boot odometer might say
five, maybe six digits by now
I would polish them
out of respect
were there anything left to polish
It's been four decades since i last did so
when they passed inspection
onto the day's work
breaking them in
creating blisters
callouses
wearing down the tread
the heels, the toes, the laces
traveling toward something
routine and labor intensive
something i did not want to do

They know my feet better than i do
supporting my arches as i fall in step
ready for another mile
around the globe
if i could go that far

I would be buried in these boots if i were to be buried
I would like to see them in a museum as a sound example
of classic footwear from our era
Upon reaching my last mile i would love to give them
to some snot-nosed punk
with 10 & 1/2 sized feet
on his way to jail and tell him. . .

Hell, i wouldn't tell him anything
i'd just give him these boots

Fourteen men in a twelve man cell

The fluorescents rise humming
Keys rattle
From the far end of the hall where we can't see
comes the breakfast cart
Our twelve man cell is full with fourteen
Fourteen men with at least a dozen excuses

Two tiers of metal bunks and plastic mattresses
and two come latelies
who shove their mattresses under the bottom bunk
to free up the aisle, the runway
for pacing men with no where to go
access to the stainless steel toilet with sink and no seat

We line up as the bars roll back
enter the day room
A few remain wrapped in scratchy blankets

The t.v. goes on
and will remain on into the night
Sometimes as punishment
they turn it off
herd us back
slide back the bars
cut our space in half
Fourteen guys who smell
are mostly morons
have bad teeth
oily skin and hair
with artless tattoos
LOVE and HATE
on their knuckles
skulls and dragons
swastikas and cartoon women
they flex to life
with solitary muscles
and roll yer own smokes

hanging from their mouths
shitting in public
masturbating under cover
bearded and dirty
constipated
with atrophied muscles, hungry for air
dreaming of that someone they will see
dreaming of their return
dreaming of a better version

The food would be punishment enough
without these days and nights of
Starsky & Hutch
Cagney & Lacey
Laverne & Shirley
Happy Days
and McGiver
busting out of impossible places
with only a paper clip
We have no paper clips
we would only stab each other
if we did

Report card

Larry continues to make bad use of time
He has shown himself capable on occasion
but is generally too playful and distractible
to accomplish much
He seems unsure of basic math facts
and processes
He has trouble settling down
He lacks self discipline and self direction
He is working far below his potential
this can be attributed to the fact
he feels it unnecessary to complete daily assignments
He is a poor citizen

Little has changed
since third grade
when it began to get dull
and the girls, interesting

My teacher's assessments
were all dead on
Only one thing
I forgot
to tell them all
to FUCK OFF

not sure if i did
or not
but for those
i may have forgot
this is for you

The Laundry

We return like old shirts
hung and left to dry
easing out the wrinkles
absent buttons exposed
pockets sewn shut

Where the drugs would wear away
and unconsciousness might intervene
atop a plastic mattress atop a concrete slab
a burlap blanket and stiff starched sheets
the crapper but an arm reach away

Where it stunk of chartreuse
and stale Camels
and the door was locked and the barred window open
and the light was never on but never off
with no wind or air
while things clank and echo, clank and echo

And a tv is on from somewhere
and a radio is on from somewhere else
And crazy Eddie has been screaming for the past 3 days
but usually it is never too loud here
and always it is never quiet

Cell #1 is jacking off and cell #2 is doing push-ups and cell #3 is
reading about Al Capone and cell #4 is listening as cell #5 tells war
stories to cell #6 who has t.p. jammed in his ears. . .

These young immortals
too many hormones, too much passion, zero introspection
seized with uncontrollable urges
cast upon a riptide of impulse
within this tight closet of forced order
pressed back into presentability
with all those labels we tried so hard to lose
reinstated and double-stitched

The True history of Bonnie & Clyde

You know Bonnie & Clyde
didn't look like
Warren Beatty or Faye Dunaway
or even Ted Bundy

By all accounts
Clyde was more homely than Son-of-Sam
and as twisted as an oversexed terrier
but he knew how to drive

Bonnie could have been Jean Harlow
with the proper rinse
and a bit more in the tit depot
A mere waif of a girl
95 psychotic pounds of unsatisfied flesh

Ray Hamilton rode with them for awhile
but mostly he just rode Bonnie
while Clyde licked his fingers
Ray got out just in time
only to get it somewhere else

W.D. Jones serviced both of them for awhile
Brother Buck and wife Blanche maintained distance
No one could keep up with Clyde's drive
and whatever it was that kept Bonnie in tow

Career-wise they made less than 20 grand
Their victims equaled Clyde's 25 years
They were the recipients of 167 bullets
Their riddled car toured the rest of the decade
without them

Clyde knew his way through the backroads
but never where they were going
Some 30 odd years later he would have been pleased
the movie would get it all wrong

John Dillinger lives

unlike Elvis
unlike J. Edgar
unlike little Melvin Purvis
who watched that night
outside the Biograph
where Manhattan Melodrama with Clark Gable played
waiting for JD to exit arm in arm with the lady in red
Anna Sage
who was supposed to set him up
but maybe she was setting up the FBI
maybe J.Edgar was setting up the American people
Gee man, it wouldn't have been the first time
would it?

Whomever they shot outside that theatre
and photographed on the slab
had brown eyes
Dillinger's were blue
The FBI explained the altered physiognomy
had occurred through plastic surgery
but none of J.D.'s documented scars were on the cadaver
who was shorter and heavier and had a rheumatic heart condition
which would have prevented him from being in the navy
or playing minor league baseball
or leaping over bank counters
Only the prints
as provided by the FBI
lined up

Only four months before this staged execution
J.D. had escaped maximum security using a bar of soap
carved to look like a pistol
J.Edgar's lace panties were in a wad

Do you suppose just maybe
crime did pay
and that J.D.
the most successful bank robber of all time

got away just like he said he would
caught up with Butch & Sundance
leaving D.B. Cooper somewhere to follow
and if so
whose massive member is that anyways
in that jar of formaldehyde
that lives in the basement of the Smithsonian
that J. Edgar used to like to dress up for
wearing stockings and heels and a modest veil
so he wouldn't look like a common whore
and that he'd spend the evenings with
those nights Clyde was out of town
or the 6 or 7 presidents who employed him
who, as time went by
were less apt to ask
 J. Edgar
what have you done for us lately?

Billy the kid

His voice thunders from across the road
all vowels, no consonants
a hateful barrage of pain-filled fury
surefire madness and a pinch of glee

An LA Dodger's cap pressed over his spongy buoyant hair
frayed cut-offs, thigh high white socks, sneakers, no shirt
skinny boney sun-burnt shoulders
knobby knees, deep clavicles, visible ribs, a pot-belly
a free-ranging wiry beard, rising and spilling
like rebellion across his enraged face

Scurries up the sidewalk like a runaway limerick
never to conclude, presses doorbells
flips off on-coming traffic, screams at
imaginary people, draws his fingers
like a gunslinger with endless ammo
spraying on-coming traffic with phantom bullets

I watch him karate kick a trashcan
admires it as it rolls and spills its shit
across the parking lot of the Fred Meyer
transfixed momentarily by his unlocked power

I'm happy for the steady stream of traffic
that keeps him pinioned four lanes over

The other good thing about him is
he keeps moving
commanding my attention
as he swaggers and staggers easterly
toward the Cascades, a bright white wall
against a stunning light blue sky
screaming incoherent invectives all the way

another reason to hate the Dodgers

The Burning stable

It's cold beyond this manger
beyond the red licking ribbons
ten horses penned, trapped
their large lush eyes wide with terror
A menacing orange glow billowing thick within
corrupts the icy void and calm grey sky
A rough hewn fence separates them
from galloping mad among the icy tundra

The white one in front may have a chance
The dappled gray, the red and brown, the rest. . .
will likely lose this war
Their hooves, head, body mashed tightly against the posts
wedged in by their own indomitable strength
panic-filled and pressed
roasting from the rear

You can hear them whinny, high pitched and shrill
snort and stomp, writhe in their attempt to escape
Small minds scrambled in self-preservation
irrevocably hell-bent toward destruction

Beyond the promise of another day
beyond the confines of the ornate golden frame
where lies the master's unseen house?
asleep? gone to town? somehow the source
of this disaster?
beyond the smoke and fire
in that harsh liberating frost
beyond this well-built fence
they're dying to break loose
and trample us where we stand

*Based on a painting from the permanent collection at the Frye Art
Museum, Seattle, WA: Adolf Schreyer, 1828-99, oil on canvas.*

Betrayal

He's getting neutered tomorrow
and we're both on edge
It's too late for him
too early for me
What better time to drink with yer tom
prior to his becoming tomless
Of course he's not much of a drinker
I've given him a cat-nip toy
which for the most part goes ignored
And I can't feed him
so he knows something's up
Returning from the kitchen with another beer
he goes for my feet
lunging with playful vengeance
I know how Judas felt
And the beers and attacks keep coming
as we lick ourselves in all the hard to reach places
and wait
for the tendrils of morning
to bleed across the sky
at which time
we'll both wake a little short

In my car

i am king tut, Yertle the turtle, the grand pooh bah
i am in control behind the wheel
i am 5 years old
i am master of my domain and first recipient
to an infinite array of tragic possibility
In my car
i am superstitious and religious
cursing god and praying the next
with one eye in the rear-view mirror
driving by faith and guile
and no insurance
looking past St. Christopher
a wind-up silver parking angel
a tiny green rubber duck
and Satan dangling in my blind side
All the debris of the world has come to roost
in my car
living testament
that after 4 years
it can get no more filthy than it already is
In my car
radio right-wingers pound it home
pontificating platitudes
daring me to call in
if i only had a phone
not in my car baby
'cuz my car is all about getting from points A to B
'cuz my car
is all about me
and, man, we both need work
and have accrued a lot of miles
and can still get it up
without Vavoline or Viagra
So let me by
i got places to be
and more than likely
you are in my way

The Marx Brothers play Auschwitz

They headlined the coveted next to last position
The earlier acts had died

Harpo with horn raced in
dropped sticks in lieu of knives
hung his leg on an SS guard
strummed his harp
just before they shot him
he gookied the audience
The crowd was hungry
but not for him
Groucho, hearing the shot, entered
The walk was there but he had to hold up his pants
He mimed a cigar
his glasses were in a pile somewhere
but his signature grease painted stash and brows were in place
if not his wayward eye
looking for an exit

Is the war over? Is it time to go home?
I was dreaming Herr Schicklgruber and I were in the showers
together. What Herr Schicklgruber was doing in the showers I'll
never know. Say, what do Heinreich Himmler and a pizza have
in common? I don't know, but I'll tell you when I eat one. And
speaking of food—how can one not—there's a rumor that red
triangles are receiving 3 squares a day—which is funny if you think
about it, so I'm sure none of you will. I don't know if it's the food
or the service, but there's a rash on my wrist. If I look close, I see
my number is almost up. And while on the subject of barbed-wire,
did you know the quickest way out of here is the farthest from our
minds. Allow me to shed some light on this, or rather, some skin on
that light. Well you're a tough crowd. From where I'm standing the
view stinks, or is it the latrine I'm looking at. Hard to know what I'm
looking at but whatever it is it's looking better all the time. . .

Chico wheeled out a little stand-up Steinway
Steinway your way, we all pray for D-Day. . .
and launched into a number that would have brought the house down

had Allied bombers not beat him to it
Groucho knelt beside Harpo, cradled him in his arms
They had slayed them in Hoboken
killed them in Newark
were world famous throughout Philly
from the Alleghenies to the Catskills. . .

Chico finished and grimaced a smile
collapsed on the keys
Groucho waddled round the Steinway:
What happens when the master race masturbates?
They finish in a hurry.
I hear there's 6 million laughs out there but I'd settle for a live one.
Alright—since our mime is dead, guess this:
Groucho stood on his head
Give up?
Mussolini.
Shots rang out, the curtain fell
Somewhere god was laughing
but where and at what no one knew
The Stooges rushed the stage
There more than 3 of them
and they weren't funny either

Notes toward greater understanding: 1) Red triangles were political prisoners— the
upper hierarchy in terms of preferential treatment. 2) Schicklgruber was purported to be
Hitler's real father's name. Hitler, a bastard, took his step father's name, as the former
sounded suspiciously Jewish. 3) Mussolini was strung up by his feet after his disgruntled
compatriots killed him. 4) Vaudevillian headliners always appeared second to the last.

Comfort food

They were sad enchiladas
Everything in them was near rotten
Make 'em hot and mean enough
and rotten doesn't matter
While i diced and cut, she told me she was going to move
It wasn't me or my cooking
she just had to get her life together
She would return to school or something
Something to make the world
or herself in that world
better

I steamed the crusty tortillas to resiliency
Calmed the soured picante with canned sauce
Fried the greenish beef
Sliced mold from the sharp cheddar

She told me she would live in Irvine at her mother's

I stirred last night's rice with last week's beans
loaded each tortilla
folding them neatly
in a pyrex dish
slathered in sauce and
placed them in the oven
We listened as they boiled over and hissed

Later
We sat down to eat
They're good, she said
and had another

What if

If Goya had used watercolors
If Van Gogh had been famous
If Stalin had entered the ministry
If Hitler had attended art school
If the Pirates had signed Castro
If Washington had been a pacifist
If King George had not been crazy
If Groucho had been an only child
If Karl Marx had been wealthy
If Freud had been well endowed
If Darwin had not sailed
If Lincoln had not attended the theatre
If Napoleon had been tall
If Custer had been patient
If Jefferson had not bought land
If Kennedy had not been handsome
If John had not met Paul
If Keith had not met Mick
If Laurel had not met Hardy
If Stanley had not met Livingston
If Einstein had been an imbecile
If Shakespeare had been illiterate
If Hemingway had not gone to war
If Dostoyevsky had been shot
and if Garfield had not

If you had gotten off the phone
and not scorched the pan
and burnt the artichokes

Well, who knows how things might have turned out

Insomnia

When you've slept 4 hours in as many days
without drugs
except for those that are supposed to induce sleep
you begin to wonder
You crave unconsciousness as much as the next guy
Her with head poised on pillow
her black hair everywhere
lips apart
a delicate rhythmic snore
that would never keep you awake
could you ever to get to sleep
And you've read all you can stand
juggling 3 books
none of which will keep you up
or put you out
You rise and the night is cold and the heat is off
and you already know there's nothing on tv
there is no one to call
and you can't type or play music
And it's only a few more hours 'til the
harsh light of morning streams in
when it will be time to DO THINGS
and it will be the 5th day
and maybe you'll start to see auras
speak in tongues
laugh at things not funny
cry for no good reason
And wonder whether insomnia
is the opposite of death
or is so far removed
as to have come full circle
These are your thoughts as you roam the house like a shark
looking at the clock
staring at the horizon
checking your pulse
in case you've already passed
on to the other side

Timing

Even before i knew the word
i pitied adults
my father and mother supporting me
jobs they didn't like
working for people they didn't like
working toward some elusive time
when they wouldn't have to work at all
and just bide their time 'til death
When, in the meantime
everything that could go wrong would
They'd lose their hearing and hair
their vision
things would grow out their butt
or neck or inside where
you wouldn't know it until it was too late
while she or he
would lose their physical appeal in umteen million
creative derogatoritive ways
'til they wouldn't care anymore
And children would come and go
And pets would come and go
And love and desire and hunger would all go go go
like the sum of all life's wants were fodder
for some cosmically cruel January white sale
leaving one without even the ability
to know when to exit
when knowing when to leave
is perhaps the only thing
worth knowing at all

Insulate

Insulate me
wrap me in gauze that'll preserve my breath
Insulate me from the machines that work the machine
the mechanical people they manipulate
places that never see the sun
churning on automatic pilot
My sight's not ugly it's the view that stinks
My aim's fine only the target keeps changing
Keep your eyes low, your steps quick
     This used to be something else
     this used to be something else
     this used to be something
Crazy Horse has been committed
Yosemite Sam is the reincarnation of Custer and Teddy Roosevelt
who lost the battle and tossed in the war
called in the 5th due to rain
Insulate me
Will work for beer
Seizures at 7
Ending up in other people's pictures
suffering home team advantage
There is no where to scream much less
anywhere to scratch your ass
Look don't touch and don't look too long
Lust with eyes shut
Table dancing worker girls on their feet
hot sweaty men on their hands
Hitler and Stalin were secret lovers who had a spat
All popes and presidents were acquitted
after god compared their crimes
with what was on tv
Insulate me in 6 feet of earth
that i may commune with worms
Insulate me with ash
We are tiny flies orbiting round metaphysical turds
weeding wishes from our day
Insulate me from the anesthetizing nettles
from fashionable hosts and floating anchors

The glue factory is taking applications
Waiting in line to get into line
Take a number and start again
Gentlemen, rev your engines and prepare to idle
Insulate me with straw, sticks, bricks
from rehashed Disney dogma
from the corporate hounds
that dog my door with self promoting altruism
FROM THE NEXT BIG PLAN
Insulate me from those with my best interests at heart
from those who would protect me from myself

Into the cold deep with cement shoes
an invincible bubble rises
and will make it to the top
wherever that is
   These days are killing me
   These days are killing
   These days
it pays
insulate

Old people
move like they have forever
like everything they had managed to avoid
had already given up the chase

That which they can't quite recall
that fizzles and fades, stops and starts
flows from time to time
when no one else is there

Old people make me impatient
a cog in the quickening momentum

Their filmy droopy eyes and cavernous mouths
gaping silent
where stories once flowed and answers came few

What is it with us?
trying to outlast parrots
with nothing new to say?
or leatherback turtles, without any plans for migration?
Holding on, tenacious like barnacles
like bats in the rafters, upside down
sleeping through their days

These blocks, these toys, no longer accessible
things that used to matter
It all once held such splendid fascination
parents faces, friends, allies, rivals, lovers
good times, bad. . . onto the flotsam
of forgotten things

These spattered gnarled hands and fingers
hinged and fused, ready to explode
this wonky reptilian stagger on into the tar-pits
searching, feeling their way through the cosmic confetti
sinking into laden footprints of forgotten ancestors
clear over to that tiny plastic toilet across the room
all the way cross the big dark unknowable room

4
Literary quite contrary

Cover letter

Here are some poems. I have read them in front of strangers, i have beaten them with sticks—the poems that is. I have pummeled and abused and turned them on their heads, laughed at them and called them names. They can stand it no more, so here they are. There is nothing you can do to them that hasn't already been done (except publish them). I hope they find refuge in your publication. If not, return them or rip them in shreds, wipe your ass with them or light them on fire (do both at once if you're up for the challenge). Send me a form letter telling me how you are inundated with thousands of NICE poems, and i'll take care of these little bastards and will kick their asses all over again.

Disclaimer

This poem is wheelchair accessible and contains no salt
This poem is not responsible for lost, misplaced or stolen items
This poem is not responsible period, but it especially does not care about
your comfort or well being, and may in fact induce bleeding, headaches,
nausea and erections lasting up to but not exceeding four hours

This poem is 87% form free and may contain improper
grammar and punctuation, meeting the USDA minimum requirement
of cliché as recommended by 8 out of 10 linguistic doctorates
from the Mumbo-jumbo letters and pretense academy
within stated guidelines, using 23% simile
assonance, alliterative affronts as well as meeting requirements
of metaphor, as written in water without getting wet

This poem will not heel but can be considered house broken
will not fetch or spray, may leap and claw furniture
plays well with others, to an extent, may bark at strangers
chase squirrels, enjoys the water and playing dead
This poem is neither fixed nor hot to breed

This poem is lint resistant, but not wrinkle free
Hand wash only, delicate spin, never use bleach
Contains no synthetic material
colors may run, rinse in cold water
do not iron, for best results, hang to dry

This poem comes without expiration date
do not refrigerate after opening
but keep in a cool dry place
away from direct sunlight
open on occasion to let vent

Contents may be under pressure
depending on how long on the shelf
contains zero corn syrup, illusions, preservatives, sweetness
or red dye # 2, may contain a scant whiff of vanilla & yellow rose extract

Aside from this, this poem is 100% guaranteed
see fine print on following page for rebate info

Primitive porn

It was long ago
Hef was dating gals his own age
Larry Flynt was exploring bestiality
in the state of Tennessee
and i was in a bookstore with my father
where we'd browse, ignoring
the *this-is-not-a-library* sign

I don't know what my father was looking at
but i had 10¢ and it was always a tough call
between Sad Sack and Hot Stuff
Then IT caught my eye
gals in ripped shirts and bras and panties and garters and stockings
tied up and strapped down
some with whips and on one cover
chucking grenades and firing machine guns

It looked like they were fighting World War Two
they were battling nazis and Japanese in any case

My father had been reading me a history of World War Two
he would read and then explain what he had read
it was all very complicated
somewhere between the failure of Versailles
and the invasion of Poland
and the dropping of the atomic bomb
there was a lot to cover
but i don't recall anything about these women
obviously brave and courageous
and pretty well-fed too
with their clothes giving out in all the right places
for it was better to imagine those places
along side those exposed areas
bound by rope and chain
tattered and bruised and desperate with just a dab or hint of blood
leered at and slobbered upon
by buck-toothed Japanese in glasses
stocky krauts with scars and eye patches

One didn't need to be an historian
or even an adult
to know what this war was about

And as soon as i began to look
i knew i wasn't supposed to
I could only imagine the fate of the girls
and whether i ended up buying Sad Sack or Hot Stuff
i could not forget these tough gorgeous women
these victorious vixens
who looked nothing like mom
or my friend's moms
or my teachers or
sunday school teachers
or the girls at school
or anybody on television even
nobody looked like these women
who were of course illustrations
but oh-so real
so very real

World War Two was a lot more interesting than dad or
Winston Churchill had been letting on
and maybe that particular war was over
but a new one was beginning
and i had but a few more years
to prepare

This big giant novel

is so long and large and dense
with hundreds of pages and
tons of chapters and sub chapters
sections and subsections and
characters, with a main guy, of course
and a girl, gotta have a girl
though she doesn't come in
till a third of the way in
Together they're trying to
accomplish this big mission
which is why the book is so
long, because this thing is
very involved and requires
thousands of words to describe
the enormity of this elaborate
adventure, you, for some reason are
compelled now to endure

With the book itself, heavy
seven, eight, ten pounds perhaps, so
heavy you rest its heft upon a pillow
upon your chest and with much
shallow breathing, grip with both hands
lest it fall and crush you
Such a large hunk of pulp it cannot
be taken anywhere, but like an anvil
rests beside the bed, holding your attentions
hostage, this large thing by Stephen King
with its all-monopolizing life-halting
nature, as other books, not quite so vast
nor grand, lesser books perhaps, or at least
less book, accumulate, vying for attention
crying out collectively for
greater volubility, please hurry
hurry through your big heavy tome
read us next, and see us home

Preparing my grant

up at an absurd hour
thinking about the grant
due later that evening
hating myself for having put it off

but those questions
those goddamn stupid questions
are they after artists or auditors?
bohemians or bureaucrats?
Thinking about my support materials
how they will stack up against
the other applicants
Thinking about the future
about my miniscule job and moneys
escalating costs
my crappy almost-had-it-car
my age
its age
her age
the woman i live with
hearing the floorboards creak above
and her dresser rattle
The novel i should write
the novel i will probably write instead
about the workshop i should take
Aren't there enough books already
enough writers
they'll be other workshops, that's for sure
they'll be other grants
a bevy of belittling grants
with enough strings attached
to hang yourself
a wide array of faceless bored members
yawning as they pick up YOUR support materials
reading them while thinking
about their cars
their wives and husbands
their own stories and failed attempts
the ones they tell

the ones they cannot
checking off the list
with a blue pencil
gone dull
an X or an O
tossing them into one pile
or another
before picking up the next

I really should get on it
the application, that is
suddenly i long to clean the house
watch Oprah
cook enchiladas
take a walk
read the newspaper

I make coffee and settle down with a book
of mysteries
a library book
and having read several pages
i find an old booger
on the page
someone else's support materials
I scrape it off and it falls somewhere
where i no longer notice it
anonymous
taking with it
my opportunity
to reject it

On the house

En route to the reading
i heard, then watched a woodpecker
It had a bright red head and striped wings
and tapped for me
I saw a pair of flower beds
big brass bed frames fencing in a garden
leaving no doubt as to the pun intended
I saw a pretty girl raking leaves, who said, HI.
A jogger girl, who nearly ran me over
An ambulance blaring its siren
going up Madison on the wrong side of the road

I entered the reading
Took an armchair beside Luke
exchanged Hi's with the old grizzled cuss
Eric Miller reintroduced himself to me
What a sweet kid
had i been as cool as that when i was 19. . .
A woman i hadn't seen before poured coffee
as i got some water
Gave Mac a whack on the shoulder
Tom took stage, things began. . .

Charlie was reading Hemingway
when Luke went for the bathroom
Robert Jordan this, Robert Jordan that. . .
There was a racket in the head
I thought Luke was making some statement
in regards to Charlie's reading
Luke came out flailing his arms
Bad mime from where i sat
Robert Jordan, Robert Jordan. . .
Luke went in, came out, went in
made another gesture
all of which Tom missed
Robert Jordan was receiving rifle instruction
as Luke huffed past where i was sitting
grabbed his coat and bag

grumbled that someone was shooting up in the bathroom
and left
Was he pissed about illicit drug use?
being left out?
that he couldn't get into the stall?
Or was it something Robert Jordan had done?

After Luke left
the strange woman came out
I could see the junk all over her
as she shuffled over to the couch and sat

Others read or played their guitars
I read my 3 or 5
the heroin-high woman read
her first time there, she said
Packed with cliché
and Johns
John John John John John. . .
10 clichés and 22 Johns later
she bid us a weak heroin farewell

Tom played a computer cartoon he had made
Eric Miller sang and played guitar
and things soon concluded
another reading come & gone

giving voice to the voiceless
words to and from the illiterate
a stage for us without a platform
space when there's nowhere else

we come here
and why the hell not
every monday night
we come here

At the Magazine release party

It happened again at the reading last night
where i went to listen and not be heard
A magazine release party, they hadn't taken mine
but i'd had had some luck with them in the past

A good crowd for poetry, though half were there to read
The curator was a good poet, told jokes, kept things moving
introduced the poets, one after another
who read their well crafted, well honed words
most of whom suffered from a severe lack
of stage presence or mic know-how

And people, sometimes sensing closure, applauded
or not, as these poets delivered their subtle
gentle imagery, a bevy of sunsets and birds and ocean tides
metaphors massaging some kind of meaning
most of which was lost on me, not one poem about
fucking or fighting or drinking or even baseball
no theft or murder nor honest crime, few seedy
revelations or guilt. . . just endless drizzle
upon the undulating flowers in grassy fields with
maybe a fence post or cow bell sounding in the distance

I thought about my numbing ass upon the hard metal chair
as one poem bled seamlessly into the next

I did not buy the magazine but was first out the door
The rain had turned gnarly and nasty, stabbing sharply
upon my lack of hat and coatless shoulders
I found my truck and drove and was forced
onto a detour along the way
taking me from my usual to a dark road
unfamiliar and winding with lots of pot-holes
I swerved to miss a opossum
and paid careful attention
all the way home

On break at open mic (4 Luke)

The bearded bespectacled beret-wearing
big-round-the-middle
poet aficionado
complains about the lack
of respect
our particular venue has
for the spoken word

Earlier this evening we witnessed
Charlie attempt to read
Robert Browning
whose meter he ransacked like a Hun
whose rhyming couplets he butchered like Hannibal Lecter
whose very meaning he dismembered like a surgeon with palsy
but this breezy assessment is not fair
to Huns, fictional serial killers
or doctors plagued by disability
as even the meanest mofo with ham-hock sized mitts
and blunt cleaver
could not do
to R.B.'s verse
what Charlie did

I respect the old critic
leaning into his cane
careful as he lights a smoke around his wiry stash and beard
He never reads his own
but on occasion will read one of the dead ones
name dropping the obscure
keeping memory of their memory
alive

Open mics coast to coast would benefit from more like him
One Charlie per venue as well
to help determine how far we've come
where we've been
and how far astray
we still can go

The Mentor

My old writing teacher
older now
and plenty old then
hunched over his beer
Wrinkles rise between the rim of his glasses
and the brim of his cap
his keen eyes observant
through thick reflective glasses
that overwhelm his short sharp nose

He is working on something
and can't get an agent
his old one died or something
he can't really drink or smoke anymore either
He said he had writer's block 5 years once
having quit cigarettes
I don't know what else he can or cannot do
He cannot stay and has to go

He knows i have adopted him
perhaps he is honored
or annoyed
but he has always been a good teacher
and like the bubbles in our pitcher
he rises to the occasion

You keep going, he orders.
You keep at it and fight those bastards.
You do it because you must.

He stands
his small wizened body towers
I stand as well and nearly topple
having sat too long on one leg
wobbly from drinking that
which he cannot
He catches me and we share a clumsy embrace

He exits the dark bar into the day
and i have another
to him

Something linear

Once there was a girl who wanted a plot
Get that book away from my side of the bed, she said.
I don't want another story that noodles along.
She was reading Zade Smith, he was reading Murakami
I want a story that goes somewhere and doesn't just diddle itself.
For that was pretty much what he told her the Japanese author did
In fact, at one point, he said, *I love the way he,* meaning Murakami,
can write about nothing, kind of like an episode
of Seinfeld, only. . .
Yes?
not funny.

He should have given Murakami a better build-up
Maybe this was why no one had ever asked him to write a cover blurb
(that and he was utterly unfamous)
or why none of his pitches for what he had produced
had garnered much enthusiasm
Everyone, including the woman he considered his better half
wanted crisp beginnings, neat endings
a love story, a tale of death, clues, whatnot. . .
heavy on the whatnot
regardless, things had to happen
you can't just contemplate the existence of god
for hundreds of pages like Dostoyevsky, or
admire your big toe through a narcotic gauze
like Burroughs

It was why the world was in trouble
Too many people doing too many things
even literature, a seemingly inactive past-time
setting up an arena in one's mind where you could watch
lions eat Christians, and not only that, but had to know
WHY, and even have it mean something, something other
than lions crave dinner like Christians require martyrdom

Meanwhile, bones and carnage litter the dry hard yellow earth
janitors, gladiators, groundskeepers, cheerleaders take the field
the crowd continues to watch with indecisive thumbs
hungry for something, chanting for more

Fungo to the dogs

It's like they were balls
and all i have is this little plastic bat
and i bat the balls clean
but its a huge field
and there are thousands of fielders
mostly milling round the infield
and i am not the only one up
in fact nobody is up
as everyone is up
we're all just fungoing with random abandon
Some have D.H.ers hired to bat for them
and this gets the attention of the big boys
out by the warning track
Esquire, Playboy, New Yorker, The Atlantic Monthly. . .
But the rest of us just have these crappy plastic bats
and we're all looking for a hole
And there are many batters and too many shortstops
and little makes it through
in fact there are so many fielders they don't even have to field
they just set down their coffee or beer
glove the ball and sit on it
like a chicken with an empty appointment book

In the mean time i'm not supposed to bat the same ball
to another fielder
it must sit under some big hen's ass for months on end
losing freshness and topicality
until this overcrowded field
realize they possess too many balls
and must toss some back

I keep spraying the field
keeping track of my balls
creating new ones
while they sip beverages
with one eye on the score board
weighing out all the other little piles
against their own

Tolstoy

Tolstoy was big
too big for mere poetry
too big for little magazines
in whatever form they existed
His short stories were never short
He wrote big heavy weighty books
with big heavy weighty characters

His own era could not contain him
whatever Rasputin, The Czar or Kaiser, Victoria or Edward
were up to
was not important enough for Tolstoy's quill

This modest-sized author
with the ZZ Top-sized beard
did not write literature
he was literature
Dostoyevsky might equal him in theme
Balzac, perhaps in volume
pedestrian meringue by comparison

The only work—and work it is—to rival
War and Peace is Les Misérables

The Hunchback, however
is no match for Anna Karenina

Perhaps if Dostoyevsky, Balzac and Hugo
ambushed Tolstoy in an alley. . .

otherwise Leo kicks everyone's ass

or, to paraphrase a different source:

Leo Tolstoy's still big
it's the books that got small

A Movable snack

Oh Ernie, we all long to be you
to write the clean sentence, cleanly
to have eaten what you have tasted
to have been in no less than 5 wars
and never lack material
yet still bore us with tales
of fishing & bull fighting & big game hunting
To have lived in the time of big game to game against
Kilimanjaro with its still pristine snow
To tramp Cuba and singlehandedly invent Mohitas
Arm wrestle Castro with green stuff in your teeth
When men were men
and women
your own invention
With but one theme you beat like a threadbare tambourine
With Europe & America still reading the little story in big magazines
Hangin' with F. Scott, Ford & Joyce & Gertrude & Gary Cooper
manly guys, and others—you were all (mostly) manly guys,
thriving in a manly world with cast iron balls that clanked as you
swaggered
and whether it was Key West, or Paris
or Ketchum Idaho
you always knew who you were
and when you couldn't be that anymore
you knew what to do

We all want to be you Ernie
or maybe we just want to know what to do
Maybe you would not have been you
had you not occurred when you did
Things being a tad more convoluted these days
and people, believe it or not
are even more crazy and F-ed-up than Scott or Zelda

A mandatory trigger lock could have denied you your date
Man, you would have really been screwed then
You could have lived, Pappy, long enough for our love
to turn on you, like love so often does
after it's been around for awhile

Shakespeare

Shakespeare often gets a raw deal
Accused of stealing scripts
plagiarizing his contemporaries
and those preceding
The argument seems to be
or not to be, that he could not have known
all what he knew to write all he did
The plays tend to be uneven
Hamlet, King John, Comedy of Errors. . .
The Histories, The Sonnets. . . The Rape of Lucrece
There was no shame 'borrowing' in his day
Originality was never the objective
neither a borrower nor lender be
may well have been a stolen line
There wasn't any money in publishing
The Bard who spelled his name
no one particular way
published little besides the Sonnets in his lifetime
The play was the thing that filled the coffers
The word was written to be heard
to entertain the groundlings
and not offend the box seats
to keep the turnstiles turning, the footlights burning
to please the virgin Queen and after her, the queenish King
while the Spanish railed, sailed and flailed on the seas
and the French, schemed and dreamed in cream-colored pantaloons

Had not some anonymous actors gathered up their promptbooks
we'd never have considered whether or not Will killed Marlowe
RADA would have devoted itself to other classic tedium
A million and one actors would have placed their stamp on other roles
Bartlett's Quotations would be an eighth of an inch shorter

and my late pal, Kent would never have climbed onto that rickety chair
in Toby & Jacks and drunkenly screamed to any and all
'Shakespeare can suck my fucking dick.'

Blame (a partial list)

First, i blame this awkward opening for which i have only myself to blame.
I blame protocol which says everything must have a beginning.
I blame you for just sitting there and beat my chest, because it's the only acceptable portion of my body i can beat in public, but it's early; ask not for whom the blame tolls, all will unfold. . .
Blame isms and Greeks, Sisyphus and rock, Aristotle and his poetics Rabelais' rants, Cervantes, Shakespeare and everything anyone has ever written.
Blame Guttenburg, Simon and Schuster, Grove Press, those who don't read and those who read too much into everything.
Blame beans, magical, gaseous and metaphorical; those who crunch fantastical.
Blame nations & Haitians, Cortez, Columbus & Custer, blame the French, Dutch, British. Blame the president, who carries the same blame as stained the one before; Blame power and power outages.
Blame hip-hop, rap, soul, country, blame the FCC & long playing LPs. Blame tv, blame You Tube and fast food; blame the waitress, blame that thing she forgot that took too long.
Blame traffic and weather, whether or not it be fair. . . Blame god, blame that which cannot blame back. Blame mom, blame dad, blame their divorce, blame 'em just cause. Blame their youth, their era, blame society and the society it keeps.
Write a poem; blame that; blame your writing teacher. Blame everyone who failed to stop you. Blame boredom and whoredom and sub standard of living standardly.
Blame the church, blame catholics, jews, christians, mormons, muslims, hindus, zoroastrians, confucians and your little buddha too.
Blame continental drift, whoever was at fault, those continents should pay more attention.
Blame cell phones and texting. Blame teenagers. Blame technology.
Blame city council, city management, underground overcosts, blame the bridge for being up and that boat that sailed belowly too slowly.
Blame the homeless. Blame and kick everything especially those without legs.
Blame congress and cronies, back scratchers, palm greasers,

midnight wheeler-dealers, ankle-grabbers, procrastinators & eager
fellatiators, legislators, floggers & bloggers, self starters, latecomers
and those who show-up on time with their own excuses.
Blame emotions, hormones, high fructose corn syrup. Blame men &
women and trannies in transition. Blame lubricants, flies in ointment,
bees in bonnets, embedded saddle burrs, open toed sandals, engine
grit, wayward pebbles, blisters, splinters, static cling, errant ball
bearings, lost marbles, waxy build-up, ripped nails, dull razors,
cold sores, artificial artifacts, esoteric heirlooms, frisky fornicators,
hyperactivity and ghosts in the machine.
Blame that smug mechanic at Jiffy Lube who said everything looked
okay.
Blame liberals, and all windbag demigods, radio ranters, easy
listening listeners, Muzak, NPR pledge drives and supporting
members like you & me.

I blame the first joint i ever smoked and that final drink i had night
before last.
I blame Alan Smoot who lived across the street and who i used to
fight every saturday afternoon because there was nothing else to do.
There's lots of blame to go around. I'd like to blame everything
i have so far failed to blame because blame seemed too easy and
obvious, a cop-out, too damn blameworthy, like lawyers for instance
or the poems of John Donne, people who wear thick coats on hot
days without sweating, vegetarians, vulgarians, tobacco chewers,
fishing lures.

Special shout out blame to the sun, moon, stars, and whomever
said Pluto could no longer be a planet. I blame spirituality, central
heating, indoor plumbing, penicillin, badly drawn cartoons,
Republicans and Ralph Nader. I blame every film ever made by John
Wayne and John Ford and those they made together i blame doubly.
I blame Hope & Crosby, Clinton's second term, rising oil prices and
falling standardized test scores. I blame fluoride, lead in the pipes,
in the paint, lead in the goalie's ass which led to yet another tie, with
four star blame to the academy for which it stands, scapegoats in the
rough, genetics in general, fireworks and the tall dry grass, hot-pants,
fish-nets, dominatrices, and a general disregard for the importance
of coasters in our society. I blame popsicles, pesticides, regicide,
patricide, genocide on ferons, freons, pheromones and a lack of

leadership among our stolen elected officials, as well as the lyrics of
Johnny Mercer and all music featuring the accordion or bagpipes.
Most of all i blame the system for which it stands especially the
Masons and other not-so-secret societies, whose names escape me,
who knew, or should have known, and should accept the lionshare
of blame, with lone exception to the pride-less lion itself, hunted and
harried, looking up from an eviscerated lamb with blood on its mane,
its face & paws, corralled by corporate wolves, while introducing
yet another lame-ass movie we've already seen, roaring twice and
pleading forgiveness for having been born a beast.

Poets

Look at all the horny drunken poets, poets
in droves, a passel of poets. . . writing and
running up bar tabs and talking, always talking
One wonders when they find the time to write
So much to say and observe and 500 times that
to read and don't forget all the events and
readings, hundreds of readings and open mics
and book and magazine release parties and
eulogies and memorials and workshops and
happenings, because things are always happening
and for a poet to write they must be a part of what is, just
as what isn't. And it's good that poets lead such rich
social lives because they earn almost no money and are
a sensitive lot and perhaps a tad suicidal—though mostly
in theory—and are prone to long walks in the rain
feeling things deeply and writing things down, lots of things
down, to get it right or just to get at it at all. And they may
be ugly or handsome or plain or pukey or rich or poor or tall or
short or missing limbs or, in some cases, have extra parts
and perhaps are both well-hung and unsung
but either way, they are sensitive, deep feeling folk
of the earth or city, and they love and hate things
deeply just as there are numerous things they revere
and hold sacred, like the written word as well as the sanctity
of the apt phrase, particularly if they're the one to have uttered it
There is a funneled pyramid's worth of poets to
inspire and enthuse from here to Homer, writers
who wrote before ink or text, just blood and time
and memory, putting it out there to affect and
infect, to make us see it like they do, to see anew, using
our eyes as they did, only through words, from epics
to epigrams from rhyming couplets to discordant free ranging rants
to haiku minimalism, with tricks or lack of punctuation, because of love

or lack of love but always some wavering measurement
in between, writing because they must, whether they are dry or
dripping wet, unleashing this torrent of infinite promise
and, failing in this, suffocating under its own
weight, sealing it with their lives, this poetic ultimatum
called life, this stuff they tell us, this thing we are

My Favorite actors play my favorite writers

I'd cast Monty Clift as Kafka
Marlon Brando as Balzac
James Dean could play Shelly or Keats or Rimbaud or Verlaine
any of that lot who died young with scant writing and loads of hair
Young Errol Flynn would make an ideal Byron
Russell Crowe could play Maupassant: The Syphilis Years
Peter O'Toole would make a fascinating Somerset Maugham

Micky Rourke would make a better Bukowski the second time
around
and could give his plastic surgeon time off
Wynona Ryder could reprise Louisa May Alcott: The Lost Adult
Years
or could play Joyce Carol Oates, providing she, Wynona, didn't
speak
All of those Merchant/Ivory gals look exceedingly literary
Kate Winslet, Meryl Streep, Cate Blanchett, Emma Thompson
Judy Davis, Judy Dench, Helena Bonham Carter. . .
Anybody with an English accent
ought to be able to write

Ayn Rand should have her own movie
I'd cast Judge Judy, i'm sure she has a SAG card

Danny DeVito could play Alexander Pope
Phillip Seymor Hoffman would make an ideal Hemingway
Capote was too easy for him
Pacino would astound critics (again) with his quirky angry surprising
rendition of Proust but would lose Oscar consideration to De Niro's
startlingly earthy James Joyce
while Anthony Hopkins amazes us (again) as Tolstoy, yes, or
Christopher Plummer
apparently already playing the part
(damn these English actors)

Surprising everyone, however, is Eddie Murphy's touching portrayal
of James Baldwin, which turns out to be the only Eddie Murphy film
without a single dick or fart joke in it

I'm uncertain as to whom i'd cast as Dostoyevsky
but Mark Twain would have to recall none other than Hal Holbrook
to reprise the role

To the following: Clark Gable, Cary Grant, Hugh Grant, George Clooney,
Rock Hudson, Gary Cooper, Sly Stalone, Arnold Swazenegger, Jimmy
Stewart, Victor Mature, Burt Reynolds, Tom Hanks, Bruce Willis, Harrison
Ford, Clint Eastwood and John Wayne. . .
Some of you could play critics
some of you could play readers
but writers?

Christopher Walken turns in an accessible, if not slightly psychopathic
Will Shakespeare—The Musical
Johnny Depp as Cervantes
Willem deFoe as DH Lawrence
and, against all type
with minimal hype
Sean Connery is Dostoyevsky
wielding a pen and quill
where he once cradled a Barreta
Dostoyevsky, he brogues, *Fydor Dostoyesky.*

Returning from a long hiatus
and a new hair piece
Bogart fleshes out JD Salinger
enigmatically chain-smoking, lisping the word, moron.
And finally, the tabula rasa of all writerdom: Thomas Pynchon
the mystery no one is prepared to take on

Brad Pitt
aiding yet another humanitarian cause
in tandem to yet another child
to his and Angelina's brood
agrees to meet the challenge
in a little picture few will see

I'll stay home and read the book

Everyone has a book out but me

All sorts of people, from a vast spectrum of interests
whether or not they be interesting themselves. . .

Formerly, mere celebrities, now, celebrity authors
Sarah Palin and Paris Hilton and her skinnier skankier pal
whatshernepotism?
Former Partridge, Danny Bonaduche and a whole slew of badly
aging child talent
the equally pugilistic, Mike Tyson—who would have known he was
a writer?
Sport legends: Joe Torre and Kareem Abdul Jabbar
Impeccable role-model athletes: Pete Rose, Jose Canseco, Denis
Rodman. . .
They can run it up the court, hit a ball & crack the keys
Ichiro has two books out in English and he doesn't even speak the
language

Various and nefarious others: big testicularites such as the
The Donald, Warren Buffet, ex-presidents. . . Valerie Plame
and even a book by the man who fingered her
That Three Cups of Tea guy, and i can see why. . .
X porn star confessionals, rock star revelations, political insiders
Even Sully Sullenberger—not sullen any longer
and Chelsey Handler, and other late night luminaries. . .

It's enough to make my bookless head spin

A category unto themselves, those prolific moralizing pundits
whose voices inexhaustibly trump the airwaves, railing incessant
upon the breakwaters of the relevant and the mundane
reconstituted rage: Savage, Limbaugh and Medved, oh-my. . .
Beck and more dreck
as told to by. . .
those no-name ghostly saps who type it up and get it out there

The suddenly insanely famous
whose legend is as fresh as their fame
and whose stories will last as long as skim milk

Those who are but mere relations. . .
Anna Nicole's mom? Mark McGwire's brother? Sonny & Cher's
daughter?
Writers? storytellers? a message to impart?

Anybody can write a book you see
it's as easy as one two. . . and then there's me
Even my friends all have books out
and they're the biggest nobodies ever. . .
i mean, look who they hang out with

No accounting for what the book buying public
if it exists, will chew, swallow or expectorate
but an argument for e-books finally becomes obvious
as an appropriate channel for all this celebrity scat
separating the natural viral fungal microbic cyber cheese
from the other stuff, for those
who have trouble telling the two apart

It's still the best smell on earth
you know
that new book smell
no matter how crappy the writing
or whoever the douchebag was
that was supposed to have said it

Someday maybe you'll see me in the bookstore
—providing they still exist—
i'm the one over there
hanging out with
the other mostly dead white guys

Sniffing books

These guys never smelled so good

One page biography

I'm an only child. My parents were as well
Both lost their mothers early, their fathers too
I was raised on a goat farm in the California
wine country. I learned to read before kindergarten
That first year of school was okay

I'm sorry i didn't go out for football in high school
I did a lot of drugs and spent a year in jail instead

I earned an MFA in theatre from Temple U.
as well as a useless BA at HSU, Humboldt County, California
I studied English & History, attended an acting academy
in my early 20s, and never graduated high school

I don't have a tv. I have a cell phone, but can barely use it
My particular form of ADD prevents
me from reading directions. Whenever
i read something, telling me how to do something
i invariably focus on how bad the writing is

I love baseball. I ache for it and the kind of weather
it accompanies. I love tigers and cats and crows
I find cooking therapeutic and have always had a fear of
starving to death. I prefer pie to cake but have no taste
for either unless i smoke weed. I love to walk
especially around Green Lake when it is sunny

I would love to do this while walking a tiger. I would
probably have a beer, because no one is going to bother
you about drinking when you're out walking a tiger

Thanks

Special thanks to Steffan Soule, (publisher & magician) Christine Marie Clarke, (editor & emotional sounding board) Duane Kirby Jensen (cover art) and the editors from those numerous publications, listed previously. Thanks also to the vast Seattle writing community and its numerous venues, particularly Bai Pai Mondays, On The House, Couth Buzzard, Hugo House & The Jack Straw Foundation.

Another variety of thanks to my mother, Jenny Cranston; my daughter, Nicky and grandson, Jadon; father, Robb Crist; contrasting grandfathers, and grandmothers & late pal Kent Schafer & writing teacher Richard Cortez Day—all of whom inspired various poems in this collection.

CPSIA information can be obtained at www.ICGtesting.com
Printed in the USA
BVOW01s1644150414

350368BV00001B/5/P